A PERFECT FIT

The Work of the Master's Plan for the Puzzle of My Life

Judy Zehr Borntrager

GROUND TRUTH PRESS

NASHUA, NEW HAMPSHIRE

A Perfect Fit:
The Work of the Master's Plan for the Puzzle of My Life

Copyright © 2019 Judy Zehr Borntrager

Published by GROUND TRUTH PRESS
P. O. Box 7313
Nashua, NH 03060-7313

I have tried to recreate events, locales, and conversations from my memories of them. In order to maintain their anonymity in some instances I have changed the names of individuals.

Developmental Editor: Brenda L. Yoder
Copy Editor: Bonnie Lyn Smith
Cover Design: Michelle Fairbanks, Fresh Design

Photographs Used by permission:
    Heritage Hall Stage: Das Dutchman Essenhaus
    Cover and Author Photographs: Rose Yoder

First printing 2019

Printed in the United States of America

All Scripture quotations, unless otherwise indicated, are taken from the Holy Bible, New International Version®, NIV®. Copyright ©1973, 1978, 1984, 2011 by Biblica, Inc.™ Used by permission of Zondervan. All rights reserved worldwide. www.zondervan.com The "NIV" and "New International Version" are trademarks registered in the United States Patent and Trademark Office by Biblica, Inc.™

Trade paperback ISBN-13: 978-1-7337677-6-7
Trade paperback ISBN-10: 1733767762

Publisher's Cataloging-In-Publication Data
(Prepared by The Donohue Group, Inc.)

Names: Borntrager, Judy Zehr, author.
Title: A perfect fit : the work of the Master's plan for the puzzle of my
    life / Judy Zehr Borntrager.
Description: Nashua, New Hampshire : Ground Truth Press, [2019]
Identifiers: ISBN 9781733767767 (trade paperback) | ISBN 1733767762
    (trade paperback) | ISBN 9781733767774 (ebook)
Subjects: LCSH: Borntrager, Judy Zehr--Religion. | Christian women--
    United States--Biography. | God (Christianity)--Will. | Trust in God-
    -Christianity. | Christian life. | LCGFT: Autobiographies.
Classification: LCC BR1725.B67 A3 2019 (print) | LCC BR1725.B67 (ebook) |
    DDC 277.3082092--dc23

Library of Congress Control Number: 2019911691

ACKNOWLEDGMENTS

Thank you to my loving husband, Myron, whose unwavering faith and belief in me gave me strength to keep writing and to complete this book. When I doubted myself, he said, "Yes, you can!" I love you, Myron Dean!

Additional thanks goes to:

Brenda,
Madelaine,
Vicki,
Joyce,
Janet,
My beautiful niece, Rochelle,
And my editor, Bonnie.

Each of you played a vital role in making this dream become a reality.

DEDICATION

This book is dedicated in memory of my father.

Jerome Edward Zehr, 1936-1990

CONTENTS

INTRODUCTION

W E ALL HAVE a story. Our story of good times. Our story of bad times. The times when God is so close and so present. The times of distance. The days of wondering, "Where are You, God?" And the days we want to re-live over and over again because our heart is so full it's going to burst! I see the stories of our lives as a gigantic jigsaw puzzle. We see all the pieces scattered about and wonder if they will ever fit together to make a beautiful picture.

It reminds me of a cute little girl I once met:

Little Anna sat sprawled out on the living room floor of her home as her mother stood nearby. At 18 months old, Anna was curious about everything. While playing with a puzzle, she struggled to fit all the pieces into their appropriate place. If a certain piece did not seem to fit, Anna would scrunch up her tiny nose, look up at those around her, and let out a howl in obvious protest! At other times, Anna would simply take a puzzle piece and give it a toss across the floor. As Anna became more upset, her mother gently knelt down beside her little girl and showed her how the puzzle pieces fit into their proper place. Anna lit up the room with a radiant smile as all the pieces came together to complete the puzzle! Trusting in her mother's guiding hand made all the difference in this little girl's world!

Isn't this situation so like us? Observing the jigsaw puzzle of our life, you and I don't grasp how the pieces will fit! We love and embrace many of the pieces, but then, there are the hard pieces, the difficult pieces. We fail to trust in our Heavenly Father's plan as we argue with Him and complain, "Hey, what are You doing? I don't want this piece. It will never work in the story of my life. It won't fit into this puzzle!" That's when we hold up a piece for God to see saying, "See this piece? I'll take that one! It's beautiful! I love it! It fits perfectly! But...this other one has got to go!" We then fling it as far away as possible, hoping to never see it again. Holding up another piece to God, we're nearly shouting as we say, "And this one, oh, You've got to be kidding me! You can't be serious?" We continue our feeble attempts of throwing away the pieces we hate. The ones we don't understand. The ones we're convinced will never work. The ones we know for certain will never fit into the story of our life.

In *A Perfect Fit,* I will share my story with you. I'll share the beautiful, the ugly, the joyful, and the sad. There are many pieces of my life's puzzle that I hated. As they were happening, I felt certain God was making a mistake, and He had to be wrong! But as you read God's story of my life, I will share how I've seen His faithfulness and how He brought the pieces together to make a beautiful picture. God placed all the pieces of my story in their rightful place in His time and in His way, just as He is doing in your story. You can trust God as He orchestrates them to be a perfect fit *every time!*

1
THE EDGE PIECES:
FAITH AS THE FOUNDATION

"For he will command his angels concerning you to guard you in all your ways." (Psalm 91:11)

I HELD ON tight. My short little legs struggled to keep up with his long strides, but I was determined to keep hanging on. Walking the streets of town in our rural, old-fashioned community, we heard the occasional *"clip, clop"* of a horse and buggy passing by. A large population of Amish, or *"plain folk"* as they are commonly known, live in my northern Indiana hometown. Since the Amish don't drive cars, a horse and buggy are their means of transportation. I always enjoyed watching them and admired the beauty of the horses. Feeling the sunshine on my face, I felt secure and protected. I knew I was safe because I was holding onto the big hands of my daddy, Jerome Edward Zehr. My hands were so little that they nearly got lost in his grip, but I was not letting go!

Growing up in the small town of Topeka, Indiana, in the 1970s was a simple way of life for my family. Our two-story white house sat on the corner of Ohio and Babcock Streets. We had a big yard with a large swing out back. I would swing as high as I could on that swing, pretending I was flying to the moon.

My mother spent hours working in the flowerbeds. Mom was well-known for her gardening talents, and people often complimented her. Our yard was beautiful with the vivid colors of many flowers. Each year, Mom made sure that a straight row of bright red petunias, Dad's favorite, lined our vegetable garden, which made a striking statement to anyone passing by!

My three older siblings and I were raised in a conservative Mennonite Christian home, where faith was central and a priority. Without fail, no questions asked, come Sunday morning, our family would be at church sitting on those hard, wooden pews, kneeling to pray, and singing the old hymns of faith—the only allowed absence being if Jesus Himself were to return!

In our Mennonite church, we sang those old hymns of faith a cappella, meaning the congregation sang without the use of any instruments. Pianos and organs were prohibited in our conservative church. The song leader, or chorister, stood up front directing us as we lifted our voices in the beautiful four-part harmony of soprano, alto, tenor, and bass. We sang gospel favorites such as "What a Friend We Have in Jesus," "Standing on the Promises," and "Wonderful Words of Life." Squirming in my seat or giggling too loudly with my cousins brought a swift pinch on the ear from Dad. And if that wasn't a cure for my shenanigans, a quick trip out the back door along with a stern talking-to and a swat on the behind from my father was quick to put me back on the straight and narrow. That's what I loved about my dad. We had boundaries and were expected to obey.

As I became older, I'd watch the clock and scowl in protest if I thought the church meeting was going into overtime. Finally, the preacher closed in prayer, and the congregation stood to sing the "Doxology," but my stomach would be growling loudly as the hunger meter registered on empty. My mother is an exceptional cook, and nothing was more inviting than to arrive home from church, walk in our back door, and smell the aroma of chuck roast, potatoes, and carrots coming from the oven, just waiting to be devoured by a family of six famished churchgoers!

As the spiritual leader in our home, every night before heading upstairs to bed, Dad led our family in devotions. Taking his Bible, my father would read a passage of Scripture and then lead us in prayer. Occasionally, Dad asked us to go around the room and each read a verse. Nothing mattered more to my parents than to know that each of their children had a personal relationship with Jesus.

It was during second grade in elementary school when I made a decision to follow Jesus; it was the most important decision of my life. After school, I regularly attended a Bible club. I loved hearing the Bible stories and watched in amazement as the teacher made the characters come alive with her flannel board! In my growing-up years, using a flannel board (a board covered in fabric) was a favorite way to tell a story. Our teacher stuck cut-out figures on this flannel board, keeping everyone's attention. On this particular day at the close of our story time, the teacher explained the free gift of salvation that was found only through Jesus Christ. Sin separates us from God, so God provided a way to Him through His Son Jesus. The Bible explains "For the wages of sin is death, but the gift of God is eternal life in Christ Jesus our Lord" (Romans 6:23), and "If we confess our sins, he is faithful and just and will forgive us our sins and purify us from all unrighteousness" (1 John 1:9). It was all beginning to make sense to me, and I recognized I was in need of a Savior.

Our teacher told us to bow our heads and close our eyes in prayer with no one looking around. She asked if anyone wanted to have a personal relationship with Jesus Christ, the Son of God, and to accept Him as their Savior. She told us, if so, then we should open our eyes and look at her. With my heart beating out of my chest so hard it felt like it would explode, I opened my eyes wide and looked right at her. On that January day in 1971, I asked Jesus into my heart to be my Savior and to forgive me of my sins. I understood that asking Jesus to be my personal Savior meant not only that He lived in me through His Holy Spirit, but also that I would live eternally in heaven with Him when I died. Even though I was young, I fully comprehended the decision I had just made. The Scripture says, "For God so loved the world that he gave his one and only Son, that whoever believes in him shall not perish but have eternal life" (John 3:16). I believed God's promise and claimed it. A happiness that I never knew began to bubble up inside of me!

Mom was there at the school wearing her coat with her scarf neatly tied in place around her head, waiting patiently to walk me home. When I finished praying, I noticed the small but very distinct smile of joy that was on her face, and yet, I was so excited about my decision that I ran on ahead! I couldn't wait to tell my dad the news! Once at home, I kept looking out the back door, waiting for his work truck to turn the corner and pull into our driveway. Finally, after what seemed like a bazillion hours in my little eight-year-old mind, Dad arrived home. As my father stood at the laundry room sink washing his hands and face before supper, I blurted out with excitement, "Guess what I did today? I asked Jesus into my heart!" With the soap suds bubbling up past his elbows and smeared across his chin, Dad stopped and looked at me. And once again I noticed a smile. I saw that same smile of joy spread across my dad's face.

A couple of years later, I wanted to let the world know that I was a follower of Jesus and asked to be baptized. My baptism happened on a beautiful Sunday morning in a country setting bright with the sun as I stepped down into a shallow creek, feeling the dirt squish beneath my feet. With my family, relatives, and members of our church standing near the creek watching, I knelt down as the church pastor baptized me with water "in the Name of the Father, and the Son, and the Holy Ghost." I knew baptism with water did not secure my salvation, as Christ already did that for me by dying on the cross for my sins. But being baptized was an outward sign of the decision I made to accept Jesus as my Savior back in the second grade. I knew without a doubt that this was a very special moment in my relationship and walk with Jesus.

This faith in Jesus was the rock on which our family stood. And it was our faith that brought us strength and comfort when life had a way of turning our world upside-down.

My Hero and Hardship

I idolized my father and believed everything he said. As a child, I fondly remember riding in our Buick. As Dad would speed up and pull out to pass the car ahead of us, I'd quickly turn around in my seat, look right at that car, and sing the jingle from a 1960s car advertisement, *"Wouldn't you really rather have a Buick, a Buick, a Buick!"* After all, if my daddy said Buicks were the best car in the world to drive, then no ifs, ands, or buts, *THEY WERE THE BEST CAR IN THE WORLD*! I trusted his every word!

Being a handyman, my dad could fix anything, or so it appeared to me! He owned an appliance store on Main Street in downtown Topeka. Zehr's Appliance sold Westinghouse stoves, refrigerators, washers, and dryers, claiming, *"We sell the best & service the rest."* He also sold Dometic kerosene and gas refrigerators to the Amish community in our town.

Dad's store stayed open until 8:00 pm on Fridays along with the other small businesses in town, and that was our family gathering spot for the evening. I can still picture my grandfather sitting by the front store window, flyswatter in hand, swatting those pesky flies that liked to hang around on a hot summer day! Those happy days and memories of time spent at my father's store are endless. Whether it was walking down the sidewalk to the local dime store to spend my weekly allowance of 50 cents, or the evening I accidently went a-slipping and a-sliding, falling down on Dad's freshly painted floor, or moments of screaming at the top of my lungs while riding with my brother on his go-kart around the track out back, I will forever hold these memories of my childhood close to my heart.

Dad loved to help people, and one of the ways he served his community was by volunteering for the Topeka Fire Department. In school my classmates would brag about their fathers, saying things like, "My dad is a carpenter!" or "My dad is a policeman!" Not to be outdone, I'd raise my head and proudly proclaim, "Well, *my dad* is a fireman!"

Being a fireman made my dad even more of a hero to me. I was intrigued with his fireman's hat, coat, and boots. His big fireman's boots sat by the back door of our house, and I would slip them on and try to walk. They came up past my knees and were heavy. I could barely lift one leg; I struggled to take a step until I eventually gave up.

One day I was walking in front of the local hardware store in town when the sirens went off. I saw the doors to the fire department fling open, and out came a fire truck with its lights flashing. I watched in astonishment as the big red truck blew right through the intersection and turned the corner. And that's when I noticed him. My heart burst with pride as there, riding on the back of the truck and hanging onto his hat, was my dad! Seeing my father in action as a fireman made me proud to be his daughter. I felt the smile on my face grow bigger and bigger as I watched my hero speed down the street.

Then one day it happened. An unexpected tragedy came without warning.

On a warm summer morning in 1973, I was in the kitchen with Mom while Dad was out fighting a house fire. We heard a knock and noticed another fireman's wife standing at our door. From the look on her face, we instantly knew something was wrong. "Jerome's been hurt and is on his way to the hospital," she said. My mind blurred as I tried to grasp what she had told us. Dad was on the roof of the house that was on fire when it collapsed and gave way. He plummeted down into the kitchen where the fire had started. Somehow, in the darkness, my father crawled to the doorway where he was found. At that moment, we didn't know the extent of his injuries, but we knew they were serious.

I raced upstairs to tell my sister who was still in bed. "Get up! Dad's been hurt! It's bad," I said. Panic swept over me. "God please don't let my dad die," I prayed! *What would I do without my dad, and how could our family survive?* I wondered. Fear gripped me. At 11 years old, I never imagined life without my father. He was the glue that held our family together. He couldn't die. He just couldn't! I found myself fiercely clinging to the hope and faith I had in Jesus.

Jesus heard my prayers. Although my father's injuries were not fatal, they were extensive. One of Dad's ankles had been crushed into 12 pieces. We learned that as the other firemen dragged my father from the fire and laid him outside, they pulled off his fireman's boots—those big, heavy boots that I played with and attempted to walk in. As the boots came off, Dad's right foot simply flopped over and lay on the ground. It was going to be a long road of recovery ahead for my hero.

A week's stay in the hospital was just the beginning of my father's recovery. The doctors performed surgery on his shattered ankle, putting in screws and a cast that came up to his hip. In the 1970s, due to hospital regulations, young children were not allowed to visit patients, even if that patient was a parent. While the rest of my family visited Dad in his room, I had to stay downstairs in the lobby. It was a long week for me as I anxiously waited to see him. My only means of communication with Dad was by using the lobby phone to call his room. The day arrived when Dad was finally released from the hospital. I impatiently watched while he was pushed to the door in a wheelchair. He gave me a weak smile. I was so ready for him to be home!

Months passed. As my father continued to heal, he wasn't able to work many hours at the store, and his appliance business suffered. Eventually Dad had to close the store down. My mother was a fulltime homemaker, and our family of six was left with very little income. I was simply too young to realize the implications this had on our household. I did not understand the burden Mom and Dad carried on their shoulders as they worried about money and where our next meal would come from. Dad struggled with not being able to provide for his family. Although my dad's faith was severely tested in this season of hardship, my parents continued to put their hope and trust in a Heavenly Father who did not abandon us.

In the midst of the struggle, God proved Himself faithful to our family time and time again. When food was needed most, a sack of groceries would show up at our door, or a check would arrive in the mail to help pay the bills. The fire department put on a fundraiser at the local high school to help cover my dad's medical expenses. To provide for our family and while still in a cast, Dad began delivering motorhomes to dealers all across the country. He would drive a motorhome to its destination, then fly back home. This new job kept him away from home for days at a time.

Unexpected Surprises

A year after my dad's accident, while he was gone on one of his delivery trips, I was playing outside on top of our picnic table. I jumped off the table and heard a loud *crack* as I fell to the ground. The first thought popping into my head was that I broke the picnic table! Trying to stand up, I realized I could not lift my left arm off the ground. I was horrified when I looked down and saw my arm bent in an awkward shape that closely resembled the letter S! I sat there and screamed for Mom with all my might. Mom came running outside to see what all the commotion was about and nearly fainted when she saw the strange curvature in my arm. Somehow, my mother helped me walk to the house with my limp, lifeless arm hanging from the socket. Once inside, my brother sat down next to me. "What happened?" he asked. Through my pain and tears, I emphatically explained to him, "I broke my arm! Don't ever break your arm! It hurts!"

The year was 1974, before 911 emergency calls were available. My mother did not have a driver's license, and since Dad was gone, the only way to get to the hospital was for my 17-year-old brother to drive me in his car. With Mom in the backseat beside me, my brother started the 12-mile drive to the county hospital. About a mile from home, in front of my uncle's house, my brother's car abruptly sputtered and died right there in the road! Frantically, my brother ran up to my uncle's door and rang the doorbell. They were home, and my uncle quickly came outside as we climbed into his car with me ever so carefully being helped into the backseat.

With my uncle driving, we once again began our journey. A few miles down the road we came to an intersection and made a right-hand turn toward the hospital. At that moment, we observed our own family car rounding the corner with my father at the wheel! He had been returning home from his trip when he spotted us and stopped the car. Mom rolled down her window and shouted, "We're going to the hospital! Judy broke her arm!"

Without hesitation, Dad jumped out of his car. Though traffic was waiting and lined up behind him, Dad raced across the road, still limping from his ankle injury, and flung open my uncle's car door. My hero swooped me into his arms as I laid my head on his shoulder. I was in pain but felt safe once again. Dad carried me back across the highway, placed me in our car, and drove us to the hospital.

My broken arm healed. Dad recovered from his accident and started working full-time again for a plumbing company. Even though he walked with a limp, I didn't care. I still had my dad. He survived a tragedy that could have taken his life. Not only did *he* survive, but we *all* survived! The outer pieces in the puzzle of my life were beginning to come together as a firm foundation. In my newfound faith, the Lord was teaching me that He never leaves His children and will always take care of us, even when we're afraid. I thought we had endured the worst. I had no knowledge of the difficult days that were yet to come.

2
THE CENTER PIECES: BEAUTIFUL MUSIC

"Trust in the Lord with all your heart and lean not on your own understanding; in all your ways submit to him, and he will make your paths straight." (Proverbs 3:5-6)

FOR AS LONG as I can remember, my family has loved music and singing, and it was a daily part of our life together. Singing is where I found my creative outlet.

As a child, I lacked self-confidence. I was very self-conscious of my conservative upbringing and struggled with the feeling of never being good enough. I was different from most people because I wore dresses every day and never cut my hair. My classmates at school would call me names and pull on the perfect, rolled-up curl of hair on top of my head that my mother so lovingly combed into place each morning; it seemed without effort for her. While I tried not to wiggle and squirm in my chair, Mother would comb a portion of my long, thick brown hair straight up and then carefully roll it down tightly with a pencil, pinning the curl securely into place with hairpins. Although others tried, nobody else came close to mastering this artwork like my mother. By the end of the day, however, the curl often came loose and ended up in a lopsided heap off to one side of my head, especially since it was such an easy target for the neighborhood kids and my schoolmates to grab onto.

I was very shy as a child. Always the introvert, I would back away and cling to the hem of my mother's dress whenever people spoke to me. But if someone began asking me questions about my favorite songs or what I liked to sing, that brought me out of my shell, and I would eagerly answer and engage in conversation.

My teachers recognized the creative abilities within me. In fifth grade, it was finally time to say good-bye to that curl on my head after I was cast as the female lead in the school play. My role as the proprietor of Katie's Cozy Kitchen in this western comedy called for a more subdued hairstyle. By sixth grade, I sang my first solo in the school Christmas concert and loved every minute of it.

Music was also a common thread among my aunts, uncles, and cousins. When visiting my grandparents' house, we would gather around their dining room table to sing while one of my aunts played the accordion, a box-shaped instrument that sat in her lap. My cousins and I loved to sit in the stairway of Grandpa and Grandma's house and play church. My older cousin was the preacher, while the rest of us took turns as the song leader. We sang many hymns we knew at the top of our lungs, with an oldie, "The Ninety and Nine," always being a repetitive favorite of one cousin in particular! We rarely left my grandparents' home without the family first singing a well-loved hymn such as "Blessed Assurance" or "Trust and Obey."

Around the age of eight, I began taking piano lessons. I was so nervous during my first piano recital! It was the middle of the summer, but somehow, I managed to tickle those ivories and complete my rendition of a Christmas favorite, "Jolly Old St. Nick." Over the years, I continued to practice and improve my ability. Dad admired my skill of playing, and it felt good to make him proud. It didn't matter if we had company over for Sunday dinner or the life insurance salesman was stopping by our house, Dad would have me sit down at the piano and play and sing something for them.

From time to time, our family sang together, giving musical programs at local churches in our area. My dad was very animated while singing. I'd watch him sing with his clear bass voice, and when going into his falsetto, he'd raise his eyebrows and stand on his tiptoes. He never stood still while singing! I not only inherited my love of singing from my dad, but also his body movements. I laugh when I realize how much I mimic him by raising my eyebrows and standing on the tips of my toes! And it truly is an impossible feat for me to stand still while singing!

Learning to Perform

When I reached high school, I joined the choir, keeping my passion for singing and my love of music alive. One of my high school classmates, Darcy, loved music as much as I did, and we sang in choir together. It made no difference to me that Darcy was blind from birth. We had so much fun singing together. It was remarkable to watch how independent Darcy was as she found her own way walking the school halls while carrying her big, bulky braille writer in her arms. Besides sharing our love of singing, Darcy also enjoyed playing piano. I greatly admired her ability to play without ever seeing a piece of music and watched her fingers move effortlessly across the piano keys. We enjoyed a close friendship during high school, but like many school friendships, we lost touch with each other after graduation.

There were many brilliant educators in our school district, but the one who made the greatest impact in my life was my high school music teacher and choir director, Miss Jones. As I struggled with self-confidence, she believed in me when I didn't believe in myself. Through all four years of high school, Miss Jones diligently worked with me, teaching me proper singing techniques and how to warm up my voice. She stretched me by offering me solos. She even gave me the opportunity to direct our junior high choir during a Christmas concert. I am forever grateful for the positive influence she had on my life.

During my senior year while sitting in study hall one day, Miss Jones came in and asked me to come with her to her office. I was puzzled since I had no idea what this was about. I followed her into her office, and she closed the door behind her. "You better have a seat," she said. She explained that the high school musical that year was going to be *The Sound of Music*, and she offered me the role of Maria. If I accepted this role, Miss Jones was going to let everyone know the part of Maria was already cast when it came time for auditions. I felt my jaw touch the floor, and my eyes opened wide. My favorite teacher was giving me an opportunity that I previously had only dreamed of! I was honored that Miss Jones trusted and believed so much in me.

I eagerly accepted the role of Maria and discovered that I loved everything about performing. This was a center piece in the puzzle of my life that took front stage as I embraced it and felt my confidence growing. Telling a story through acting allowed me to be someone else as I created a character and made her come alive. That musical was the highlight of my senior year and the beginning of a whole new world for me. With my love of music, I learned that in spite of lacking self-confidence, I was not afraid to be in front of people. I began to recognize that God gave me a talent that could bring joy to others around me. I needed to rely on His strength and to use it in a way to draw people to Him. By the end of my senior year, I realized that all I wanted to do after high school was to keep singing. But where? And how? I knew I had to trust in the path God had for me as I looked to Him for the answers to these questions.

Traveling the USA

After my high school graduation, I sought out opportunities to continue my love of singing. I had an interest and desire to sing with the Gospel Echoes Team Prison Ministry. With headquarters based in northern Indiana, this prison ministry is well known across the United States, especially among Mennonite churches since it is from the same Mennonite faith that I grew up in. The mission of Gospel Echoes is to share the love of Jesus to people in prison through Bible study correspondence courses and ministry teams that travel to prisons throughout the United States and Canada, sharing the gospel through preaching and music.

Following several singing auditions, I had an interview with the founder. "You risk your life every time you go in a prison," he told me. "Can you handle it? It's tough," he said. His words didn't shake me. I was young and determined. I wanted to explore the world and gain independence while sharing my faith in Jesus through song to people without hope. I was so excited to be accepted as a part of the ministry's volunteer singing team in the summer of 1981 for 18 months.

Our team of six people included me, three other young adults, and Glendon and Lorna Bender, our team leaders. I was excited to be on the team with Ken Miller, my second cousin. We had previously sung together in a community chorus, and it was good to be on the team with someone I knew.

I joined the team soon after my 19th birthday; this was my first experience being away from home. Our road tours were long, lasting anywhere from four to eight weeks at a time. Singing in state and federal prisons all across the United States and parts of Canada, we traveled on a 1965 Silver Eagle bus that had been converted into living quarters. After giving our musical program, we passed out Bible study correspondence courses, New Testaments, and small red address booklets to the inmates. Everything about road life was a wake-up call to me and a real education on life in the outside world. It was not easy living on the road, but it opened my eyes to the needs of the hurting and lonely.

While nervous in the beginning, I quickly adjusted to the routine of singing in prisons. At first, when the bus rolled up to the gate, the sight of these huge penitentiaries with their barbwire fences and guard towers all around gave me an eerie feeling. Our bus entered the controlled entryway of the sally port to the prison where a gate clanged shut behind us before the next one opened. Once inside the prison, however, passing through security, guards searching our sound equipment, and the loud "buzz" that allowed the doors to open and close soon became second nature to me. I learned how to tune it all out when I felt the stares and heard the whistles from inmates as we walked through the prison complex, pushing and carrying our gear to the recreation hall or chapel where the program would take place.

Our team traveled coast to coast, making stops in many of the big cities, including New York, New Orleans, Miami, Denver, Portland, and more. I missed my Indiana family while on tour, but this team of six soon became my second family. In a letter written home to Mom and Dad, and referring to Ken and a few others on the team, I wrote, "On the bus it's the same story. Brothers who just love to tease me!"

On one particular day, we had been traveling for hours, and the space in this "chariot" of ours had begun to feel claustrophobic. Glendon suddenly pulled off the highway and parked the bus along the side of the road. "Everybody get out," he said. The solution to our claustrophobia was a dose of much-needed fresh air and exercise! With traffic speeding past us, I can't imagine the thoughts of onlookers as we ran laps around the bus in a goofy fashion, even throwing in a few jumping jacks. The laughter was contagious.

This is how we lived life on the road. The bus was my home away from home, and I loved having my own little room as my personal getaway. We often drove through the night to reach our next destination. I would lie in my bed and gaze out the window, looking up at the stars as the hum of the bus wheels lulled me to sleep. Living life together, we experienced a lot of laughter and many tears, prayed for each other, and grew as a family.

Sharing the Message of Hope

It was both fascinating and eye-opening to tour the United States, singing in maximum- and minimum-security prisons. Most inmates were receptive and appreciated the programs we gave, while others were cold and aloof. And yet, we shared the same message to all through our songs and testimonies of what Christ had done in our lives, offering the hope that only Jesus can give. We witnessed many broken lives being changed and transformed by the power of God's Holy Spirit.

Most of our programs were given in the prison chapels. On occasion, we were permitted to walk the halls of the lock-up area, going from cell to cell, visiting with the inmates. One such occasion happened in a Virginia jail. Ken carried his guitar as the two of us walked together through the cell block. It was a moving experience for me to reach through the bars of a jail cell and shake an inmate's hand. We saw lonely faces and blank stares. My eyes became wet, and I silently prayed for strength to get through the song I was singing as I observed an inmate blink back tears.

In some of the larger correctional facilities, our team gave multiple programs in one day, singing in different areas of the prison. Often, when we spent the entire day in a prison, we ate our meals in the prison cafeteria, right alongside the inmates. I felt no fear sitting beside them and grew to love these hurting souls who just needed to know that someone cared. Our team met many inmates who sincerely loved Jesus. It was a great blessing for us to witness their joy and enthusiasm in spite of being incarcerated.

While sharing at a women's prison in Florida, many women responded and came forward at the end of our service when Glendon gave the altar call asking if anyone wanted to receive Christ as their Savior. Earlier that day, the chaplain told us the service was cancelled, but we were so grateful when security allowed us to come. It was cramped and tight in the room, but we crowded closely together as we stood in a circle and prayed with the inmates. One beautiful young woman told me she wanted to ask Jesus into her heart. I took her aside and prayed with her as she confessed her sins and accepted Jesus as her personal Savior. The glow on this woman's face was evident as she exclaimed, "I did it! I feel so different!" I asked her where Jesus was right now, and without a moment's hesitation, she testified, "In my heart!" I'm sure I heard the angels singing and rejoicing over us that day!

On a Sunday evening in January 1983, my term with the Gospel Echoes singing ministry team came to an end. We sang together for the final time at a church in my home state of Indiana. Singing to a fully packed church house, we shared testimonies of how God transformed the lives of many inmates over the last year and a half. But inmate lives were not the only ones changed because my life was transformed, too. There was something powerful about living life together, singing, traveling, and bringing hope to those in prison through music that made me want to seek Christ and His purpose for my life even more. I was humbled and grateful to have a small impact in someone's world through my Gospel Echoes Team experience. This piece of my life's puzzle was so exciting. My love of music and childhood faith gave me this great opportunity, and as it came to a beautiful end, I wondered where God would take me next.

The Music Continues

Nestled in the picturesque, small, northern Indiana town of Middlebury, one will find a quaint tourist attraction, Das Dutchman Essenhaus, complete with a restaurant and bakery, gift shops, and a beautiful inn and conference center. The restaurant is widely known for serving Amish-style dishes along with their delicious home-baked pies. Several years ago, this Christian-owned business remodeled one of their buildings, renovating it into a small theater called Heritage Hall. Since 2013, I've been blessed to continue my love of acting and singing at this charming little playhouse. Performing at Heritage Hall is much more to me than just entertainment. This Christian organization strives to be different by offering family-friendly shows that give a message and inspire hope. I love being able to continue sharing that message through singing and acting.

This gift of singing that God has given me has not come without testing. One of my church choir directors shared that it's not *if* our singing abilities will be tested, but *when* they are tested, because it will happen at some point in our life. For me, it happened in 2006, after my left eardrum ruptured, greatly impacting my hearing ability. It's taken two surgeries to repair and rebuild that eardrum with skin grafts, and although those surgeries have restored hearing, they have done so only partially. Because of the damage done to the ear, I'm left without one of the tiny bones in the inner ear, which unless I have further surgery to implant an artificial bone, there is permanent hearing loss. I have opted to use hearing aids and have adapted how I sing by making sure I stand close to the monitors or speakers.

I don't know why God allowed this hearing loss when the ability to hear clearly is so crucial to a singer and performer. I only know that He continues to use me in this way in spite of my disability, and for that, I am thankful. I've been privileged to perform locally with both community and professional theaters. I still sing in the church choir, and over the years, I've been in the studio, recording three solo albums.

As long as God chooses to use this talent through me, I desire to be an inspiration and long for people to see Jesus living in me.

3

THE DARK PIECES:
A HARD ROAD TO WALK

"Then you will know the truth, and the truth will set you free." (John 8:32)

A S A 25-YEAR-OLD, I longed to be married. Many of my close friends were getting married, and I was often a part of their wedding, either as a bridesmaid, playing piano, or singing. While I was honored to be a part of their special day and was excited for them, underneath my smile and the congratulatory hug there was an ache. I silently wondered when it would be my turn to walk down the aisle and marry my Prince Charming. And then, on a Sunday morning in 1987, I met a tall, handsome gentleman at the conservative Mennonite church where I was attending. After introducing himself as Myron Borntrager, I learned that he recently moved to Indiana from Iowa and was looking for a home church. Myron started coming to our church on a regular basis and joined our young adult youth group. One evening after a youth get-together, he summoned up the courage to ask me out on a date. Not wanting to appear overly anxious, I gave him a cautious *yes*. After all, since he drove such a cute little red pickup truck, I thought I should give him a chance!

Our first date was in November. Myron shared with me how he grew up in the Amish faith in a small town in Iowa and lived on a farm just down the road from Iowa Mennonite High School. I remembered that while I was a part of the Gospel Echoes Team Prison Ministry, our team would often travel right past his Amish farmhouse when we were on our way to sing at that Iowa high school. This amazed me how small our world is! That date led to a second date, and then a third. The more time we spent together, the more interested I became in this good-looking, curly-haired chap!

The relationship flourished, and we fell in love. After only three months, there was a proposal, and I eagerly said: "Yes!" We began wedding plans for the following October. As any new bride-to-be, it was an exciting time! I could hardly eat or sleep; I wanted to be with Myron every moment of every day! It was hard to concentrate during work at my office job. I'd daydream of being his wife, anxiously anticipating the time when I would finally call myself "Mrs. Borntrager"! The days simply did not go by fast enough!

Planning the wedding was so much fun. All the pieces of the puzzle were fitting together beautifully. There would be red roses, carnations, and a cake with a fountain made by my aunt. One thing I knew for sure was that there would be a lot of music! My brother was singing with a men's gospel quartet at the time, and I accompanied them on the piano while we gave concerts around our local area. It was fitting to have them sing in what seemed like my fairytale wedding!

We did all the right things a couple should do to prepare for a healthy marriage. We met with our pastor to talk about the meditation he would be giving on 1 Corinthians 13, the Love Chapter. We attended premarital counseling with a local Christian couple. We talked about children. I wanted two; Myron wanted three. We found a perfect old farmhouse in the country to rent. We seemed to be ready for this journey called marriage.

On a soggy, rainy day in October 1988, our wedding day arrived. The rain, however, did little to dampen my spirits! I stood in the back of the church waiting as I listened to my brother's quartet sing a beautiful song of thanks. Finally, my time had come, and it was my turn to make this walk down the aisle. The pianist began to softly play Pachelbel's classical piece, "Canon in D." The congregation stood as my father, looking so handsome in his blue, pinstripe suit, looked at me and held out his arm. Clutching my bridal bouquet of red roses in my left hand, I grabbed Dad's arm with my right hand and smiled. "Ready?" he asked. We slowly began making our way down the aisle. I was so ready to begin this chapter of my life.

I thought our ceremony was beautiful. It was picture-perfect in my mind. The quartet sang wedding music in melodious harmony. Our pastor gave the meditation on the true meaning of love, with God as the center of our home. It was an honor to have the leader of my prison ministry team, Glendon, marry us as we said our vows promising to love each other "until death do us part." I turned to Myron and sang a beautiful song to him about us climbing the hill together. We knelt as Glendon prayed over us, asking God's blessing on our new life as we climbed this hill called marriage.

We did not realize then just how steep that hill would be. We didn't know how difficult and how treacherous the path would become. We only knew that we were in love and could not wait for the adventure to begin! But our faith in Jesus would be greatly tested as we uncovered some very dark pieces in this puzzle called life.

Darkness Revealed

Three months into our marriage, there was a notable anxiousness and depression within me. I was filled with a hopelessness that I couldn't explain. I found it difficult and nearly impossible to communicate my feelings to Myron. This was not what marriage was supposed to look like. This was not the "happily ever after" that I had dreamed of. I would come home from my office job and start supper or do a load of laundry, but I felt very insecure in my role as a wife and never felt good enough. I loved Myron, and I had no doubt that he loved me, but I became withdrawn and did not understand what was triggering my negative emotions. There were times when Myron could do nothing but hold me as I cried uncontrollably. I was unable to communicate with him what was going on because I did not understand it completely myself. I only knew that I no longer wanted to live like this.

In the midst of grappling with these horrible emotions, while on my lunch break at work one day, I sat in my car and planned my suicide. I didn't really want to die; I simply wanted the pain to go away. Sitting there alone, I let my mind wander as I thought of my furry, black cat, Baby Roo, a gift from my father. Shortly after Myron and I were married, I noticed my dad's work van pulling into our driveway. I eagerly went outside to greet him as he opened the door to the back of his van, and there, staring back at me, was a tiny kitten. As it let out a pint-sized "meow," I was instantly in love with this teeny, black ball of fur. I began calling her my Baby Roo. This little kitten grew into a gorgeous, long-haired, black feline. I loved Baby Roo. Thinking of her as I sat in my car that lonely, awful day, I couldn't bear the thought of leaving her alone. Perhaps she wouldn't mind if I included her with me in this suicide.

Tears were stinging my eyes as I snapped back to the reality of where I was and what I had just planned. The suicidal thoughts scared me. Praise God, I never acted on these thoughts or went through with my plan. I am so thankful God had another plan. In that moment, He prompted me to call the only person I knew to reach out to—Darlene, the woman who had done premarital counseling with us.

A few days later, I found myself sitting in Darlene's office. Darlene sat at her desk and took out a book. I felt myself cringe as she began reading a list of 10 symptoms mentioned in the book. Among them were depression, fear, guilt, a shutdown of emotions, and poor self-image. Darlene went on to explain that it's not unusual or uncommon for a person to have one or even two of these symptoms in their lifetime. The room was quiet as Darlene looked up at me.

"You have all 10," she stated. I sat still and silently nodded yes in agreement.

"Would you like to know what the book is about?" she asked. Once again, I nodded yes.

The book was titled *A Door of Hope* and dealt with issues of unresolved childhood sexual abuse. Darlene told me that while Myron and I attended premarital counseling with her and her husband, she knew I would be back. During our sessions with Darlene and her husband, I spoke briefly of the sexual abuse I experienced years earlier at the hands of a family relative. While I was aware of the sexual abuse in my life, I did not identify it as something that needed to be dealt with and chose instead to ignore it. As I spoke to Darlene that day, I was shaken. For the first time in my life, I recognized that the safe childhood I remembered had a dark shadow over it that I now had to deal with. This childhood trauma I never dealt with had not healed. The only way to begin the healing process was to reopen the wound and peel off the scab—one layer at a time.

Healing

This was just the beginning as and Myron and I began a painful journey together toward healing. The process was not easy, and it wasn't going to be a quick fix.

Soon after my meeting with Darlene, Myron and I went over to Mom and Dad's house and shared with them what we were going to be facing in dealing with my unresolved issues of childhood trauma. Standing at the back door before we left that evening, I cried as Dad gave me a hug and prayed, asking for God's guidance in the path that lay ahead of us.

Over the next five years, Myron and I attended therapy sessions together, meeting with several Christian counselors and support groups. Both of us brought horrible baggage into our marriage. From his own upbringing, Myron began to deal with the pain of rejection and worthlessness he felt from years of verbal and emotional abuse. I recalled the pain of my sexual abuse by a family relative.

As a young girl, the abuse started when I went over to this relative's home as a live-in nanny to help care for their newborn baby. I would stay overnight at their house for a few days and then return home. This pattern happened over a period of two years, continuing until after a second child was born. I learned to live in constant fear whenever our family was together and my abuser was present. Not only did the abuse happen at his house but also in our family home. Whenever he caught me in a room by myself, he would violate me. He would often come up behind me, grabbing me in an intimate way that made me cringe and recoil. I begged him to stop, but he didn't. While staying overnight at this relative's home, I slept on the living room sofa. One night, I was awakened by a powerful thunderstorm. As a bolt of lightning lit up the room, my eyes suddenly caught the silhouette of a man standing next to the sofa, causing me to nearly jump out of my skin. It was my abuser, and the memories of what he did to me on that horrible night are unforgettable. I felt trapped and powerless to tell anyone what was happening.

As much as I adored my father, I did not share with him the horrors of what I was suffering. My perpetrator would continually beg me to not tell anyone, so I reluctantly complied. He and his wife attended the same church that my family did. During the week, I suffered at the hands of my abuser, and on Sunday morning he would be sitting in church, praying and singing hymns along with the congregation. I never told anyone about the pain this caused me or what I was going through. That was the power my perpetrator held over me. It was only after I returned home one evening from my abuser's home that I broke down and shared the awful truth with my parents.

My parents were notably shaken. The abuse finally came to a stop, but only after my father confronted this relative, letting him know the sexual abuse had to end. Years later, my father admitted he should have contacted the police and pressed charges. Looking back, I wish my hero father would have protected me in this way. This information should have been brought before the church with my abuser's name given so that other young girls could be protected from this man. I believe my father was at a loss, not knowing what to do. I don't hold that against him. Sadly, it's far too common for sexual abuse within the church, especially conservative churches, to be given a label of "forbidden" and not talked about or dealt with.

As my life continued, the pain of the sexual abuse and the scars that I carried were swept under the rug to be forgotten. However, my abuser was still a part of my life since he was a family relative and therefore a part of our social gatherings. Moreover, he continued to attend the same church that I did. Life for me went on as "normal," more or less. I thought I had put it behind me and went on to travel across the United States, singing with the prison ministry team. Then, after I married, it all unraveled in a dangerous downward spiral of anxiety, depression, and suicidal thoughts.

Confronting the reality of my abuse brought with it a tremendous amount of guilt. *Why did I let it continue for more than two years? What did I do to cause it since it must have been my fault somehow? Why didn't I tell anyone about the abuse? Why did it take me so long to tell my parents,* I wondered? A great amount of shame played into all of these horrible thoughts, which I now recognize as lies from Satan.

One of the first steps toward healing, encouraged through therapy, was to come face-to-face with my abuser. I was told I needed to confront my perpetrator. My counselors asked that I arrange this meeting on my own. Summing up every ounce of courage I had, I made a phone call to my offender's home and arranged a meeting. I simply asked that he and his wife come over to our house to talk.

My anxiety levels were high as the night of the meeting arrived. With only Myron, my abuser, his wife, and me present, we gathered in our family room. My heart was racing as I faced my perpetrator. Fighting to stay calm, I told him I had been carrying around a burden for many years. I explained how I struggled as I carried this huge backpack on my shoulders that didn't belong to me. I told him it belonged to him, and I was not going to claim it anymore. It was not, and never was, my responsibility.

During that meeting I "unloaded" that backpack and "laid" it down at my perpetrator's feet, stating I was not going to pick it up again. What he did with the knowledge of the effects of his abuse was his responsibility. I watched in disbelief as my perpetrator stood up and walked out of the room, denying everything I told him. For the first time since the abuse, I felt real anger toward him. *How dare he just walk out and leave,* I thought! The meeting ended, but I refused to pick that backpack of blame and shame back up. For years I struggled with feeling that the abuse was somehow my fault, and that I had caused it. But this time was different. This time I left those false feelings of guilt on the back of the perpetrator and at the feet of Jesus, my Savior. Jesus gives us His promise of rest when He says, "Come to me, all you who are weary and burdened, and I will give you rest. Take my yoke upon you and learn from me, for I am gentle and humble in heart, and you will find rest for your souls. For my yoke is easy and my burden is light" (Matthew 11:28-30). I claimed that rest and was finally free from this burden.

Though I was free from the weight of the abuse, there were still hard days ahead. I didn't know or understand why this happened to me. How could God ever fit this dark, unwanted piece into the puzzle of my life? It had devastating effects in so many areas of my life, especially my marriage.

For years, I kept throwing this piece away, hoping I would never have to see it or face it again, but it kept rearing its ugly head.

Moving Forward

A few years later, my abuser filed for divorce from his wife. I no longer saw him on a regular basis, but I learned that he was still sexually abusing girls, and there was an investigation against him. An abuser rarely has just one victim, so this news was not a shock to me. I made a call to Child Protective Services, so my name was on record as a victim of this offender. After I made that call to CPS, I received a phone call from the detective who was investigating the allegations. The detective identified himself and asked if he could speak with me. I was apprehensive, but knew I had to tell him the truth about what had happened to me.

This detective came to our house, and we sat down at the kitchen table. He began our conversation by telling me what my perpetrator was doing to a little girl. I was crushed. I had flashbacks as I remembered that this is exactly what this offender had done to me years prior. It was extremely difficult, and I had so many emotions as the detective questioned me. Barely looking him in the eye, I had to relive those awful moments of sexual abuse and to describe in detail what my abuser did to me. However, I later realized that talking in depth about my story brought even more healing that I desperately needed.

As the investigation continued, it was a surprise to see my perpetrator come to our church one Sunday morning, the same church he had once regularly attended. During the service, my abuser walked up front to the pulpit and told the congregation he wanted to share a prayer request. Myron and I sat there in our pew wondering what this man could possibly have to share with the church. My abuser told the congregation there was an investigation against him but did not explain what the allegations were. He simply stated that there were charges against him, "Of which I am totally innocent," he said. My offender asked that the church pray for him and that the charges would be dropped. I sat there astonished at what I had just witnessed. He was still denying the horrors of what he had done and was still continuing to do to innocent little girls.

Myron and I left church that day telling no one of the awful truth that we knew. (Tragically, my father was not present on that Sunday morning since he had passed away from cancer a couple of years prior. I often wonder what he would have done and what his response would have been.) As if Satan was laughing in my face, this was a time when this dark puzzle piece continued to haunt me.

My abuser was never arrested. As with many abuse cases, there was not enough evidence to prosecute with one person's word against another. I was hurt and angry when I learned that the charges had been dropped; I felt betrayed by the justice system. But, in order to move forward, I had to let go of my pain.

I began to pray for my perpetrator. As I prayed for him, I found it impossible to be angry with him, and I began to experience wholeness and a peace in my soul. I learned that while forgiveness is not easy, it is a daily choice and a process. Forgiveness did not excuse the wrong of what my abuser did to me, but it meant that the wrong done to me would no longer control my behavior. This dark piece of my puzzle would not define my future.

During counseling, I was often given the term "victim" or "survivor of sexual abuse," and I hated those terms. They floated around in my head in a way that defined me. I didn't want to be identified or labeled as a "survivor"! I wanted to be free and to be healed! A real breakthrough began when the words "I am a victim of sexual abuse" no longer consumed me. It stopped being the first thing I thought about when I woke up in the morning or when I went to bed at night. My abuser was not constantly on my mind and interfering with my day. I found I could live my life and be free from this bondage when I released him and the sins he committed against me to my Savior, Jesus Christ. Through the power of the Holy Spirit, I forgave my abuser for the acts he committed against me. This took me from simply surviving to a new place of hope where I knew this part of the puzzle would no longer follow me around.

However, I still struggled with real questions, such as, *Why did this happen to me?* and *What good will ever come of this?* I kept seeking answers to those questions. As with most dark pieces of our story, we fail to trust that God sees the big picture. The book of Romans offers a promise from God's Word that I held onto: "And we know that in all things God works for the good of those who love him, who have been called according to his purpose" (Romans 8:28). It was not until years later, while I was in another country, that I saw God so clearly demonstrate His power, and miracles happened.

4
THE MULTICOLORED PIECES: GOING HOME

"Be still and know that I am God." (Psalm 46:10)

"IS IT CANCER?" I asked. Holding the phone to my ear, I held my breath as I waited for my mother's response. While sitting in a corner office at work, the news my mother told me that day in March 1990 forever changed my life and the life of my family.

My father had just been diagnosed with pancreatic cancer. After speaking with Mom, I hung up the phone and sat there at the desk unable to move. For that brief moment in time, life suddenly stopped for me. Eventually, I summoned up the courage to tell my fellow coworkers what I had just learned. While their offerings of sympathy were heartfelt, I immediately left the office and drove to Mom and Dad's house. After everything my father had been through in his life, this news was hard to digest. I sat there speechless at the kitchen table with my mom as she cried. Still in shock from the news, Mom and I drove together in silence as we made the hour-long trip to the hospital where my dad had already been admitted.

Walking inside his room, I leaned over Dad's hospital bed and gave him a hug. There were no words, so I just hugged him and cried. True to Dad's nature, he put his arm around me and started to comfort me. "It's going to be okay," he said. But I wasn't okay. Like most people receiving the news of cancer, I had no idea how to handle it! Cancer only happened to other people. Not to our family, and certainly not to my dad!

I left Dad's room and noticed my mom's mother, my 86-year-old grandmother, in the hallway coming toward me. When I reached her, we leaned on each other and cried. With tears in her eyes, my grandma's voice cracked as she asked, "Why can't it be me?" My grandfather had died 16 years earlier; I did not have an answer for my grandma. I knew I had to trust in God's sovereignty, but in that moment, I was at a complete loss.

Cancer's Toll

About a year prior to Dad's cancer diagnosis, he complained of back pain, and soon he also noticed pain in his abdomen. He wasn't hungry and began losing weight. The doctors told Dad it was his gall bladder, and eventually he had surgery to remove it. However, instead of recovering, my dad's health continued to decline. My father's back pain was actually one of four malignant tumors growing inside his body. While he began chemotherapy treatments, the doctors didn't give us much hope for his survival. We watched as cancer began taking its toll on both my mom and my dad. My father was becoming so thin, and his skin turned an ugly color of gray. Mom was there during his treatments, but there were days when she struggled with knowing what to do or say to give my father some comfort.

A few weeks after learning of my dad's illness, I invited my parents over for a Sunday afternoon dinner. I eagerly made all of Dad's favorite foods, including meat, potatoes, and fresh strawberry pie for dessert. But cancer had robbed Dad of his appetite, and it was heart-wrenching to watch my father struggle to eat. He wasn't even able to eat any of his favorite strawberry pie. I wanted to cry because this was not the dad I knew!

In May of that year, Myron and I began building a new home on six acres of land we bought in the country. There were so many decisions to make, but my mind was a blur. My heart was not fully a part of the process of building a new home because I was brokenhearted over my father's illness. Myron was left with a lot of the decisions, including the design and layout of the home. We did most of the work ourselves, which meant that

Myron worked many evenings installing the plumbing, heating, and electrical.

As July Fourth arrived, we took the day off from working on our house to be with extended family in my hometown of Topeka for its annual celebration. It was an honor that my parents had been chosen to be the parade marshals that year. We lined up to watch the parade along Main Street, and we spotted Mom and Dad riding in the back of a red convertible. Dad looked pale, weak, and very thin as he smiled, waved, and threw candy to the children. Despite my father's haggard appearance, I was never more honored to be his daughter. I believe I loved my father more in that moment than ever before. In the midst of his pain and suffering, he was still caring for others and being of service to his community.

After the parade was over, our family gathered at my parents' home to wait for the evening's fireworks that we could watch from their yard. My father walked me across the lawn and put his arm around me. "Jude (his nickname for me)," he said, "No matter what happens, I've always been proud of you." I felt a lump forming in my throat. I knew what Dad was facing in the morning.

The following day, on July 5, 1990, my father was admitted to the hospital to have a simple procedure done. He had jaundice, and the oncologist wanted to insert a tube to drain Dad's liver. However, complications arose, and things did not turn out the way we had planned. Dad did not bounce back, and as the days turned into weeks, his doctor finally told us that Dad would not be leaving the hospital. This is where he was going to die.

Living in Grief

Myron and I continued to work on our new house while also preparing to move out of our rented farmhouse by the end of the summer. I strove to keep on with life even though I was tired, and most days I didn't feel like it. I hated cancer. I watched as my strong, six-foot, two-hundred-pound father became just a shell of a man, wasting away to skin and bones. Watching someone you love battle a terminal illness is both emotionally and physically exhausting. Your life is turned upside-down. One day I would be working at the new house, and the next day I would be sitting at Dad's bedside in the hospital. It was a daunting and overwhelming time, and it's still a blur to me how things got done.

When I went to the hospital to be with Dad, a vivid and sad memory sticks out in my mind of taking the elevator up to the sixth floor where the oncology unit was located. As I stepped off the elevator, I heard moaning coming from down the hall, and I knew it was my father. Although his caretakers were giving him the highest dose of morphine possible, it still did not take away his pain. It was so difficult to watch Dad suffer. Often when I walked into his room, Dad would raise up his arm, and I would sit beside him on the bed and take his hand in mine. One day while holding his hand, it suddenly hit me. I had flashbacks of holding Daddy's hand while walking the streets of Topeka as a child. I couldn't stop the tears. I wanted to keep holding onto my daddy's hands forever. I never wanted to let go.

I grieved seeing my father in this condition. I longed to have my big, strong dad back, the one who taught me about Jesus. While I watched his outward appearance waste away, his character never changed. Through the pain of his cancer, Dad's faith never faltered. People came to visit and asked, "Jerome, how are you doing?" Dad replied with a firm "I'm on my way to heaven."

Several members of the Topeka Fire Department came to the hospital one evening to honor my father for his 21 years of service to the department. He was presented with a beautiful plaque. It was such a bittersweet moment to watch Dad's fellow firemen crowd into the small hospital room and gather around his bed. We all knew my father's days as a firefighter were over, and this was the fire department's way of saying thank-you.

A month later, Myron and I moved into our new home. It should have been a happy day, but my heart was heavy like the rainclouds that were pouring down rain. I knew Dad would never come to our new home and enjoy a meal with us or help Myron with work projects. He would never sing with me around the old upright, antique player piano that had been in my childhood home and now found its place in our new home. Moving into a new house shouldn't have all these negative emotions of sadness. Yet, somehow in the midst of our pain, we settled in and began our "new normal" of daily routines while living with this difficult puzzle piece of grief.

Saying Good-Bye

The weeks with Dad in the hospital continued to go by, and we "celebrated" his 54th birthday on August 22nd. It wasn't much of a celebration, however, as we were all aware that this would be my earthly father's last birthday. Dad grew weaker and weaker, and eventually he stopped eating. My mother wrote down the last prayer she heard my dad pray. "Dear Heavenly Father, You're in control. You know what's going on. I don't. Dear Father, I just want to be Your servant. You know what the next step is."

In the early morning hours of Sunday, September 2, 1990, the sharp ring of the phone jolted Myron and me out of our sleep. We were told to come to the hospital as Dad would soon be gone. We arrived to find Dad breathing very slowly. We watched and waited for him to leave this earth and be with Jesus. Around 5:30 am, Daddy breathed his last breath. His journey on this earth was done.

We stood by my dad's bedside, tears flowing. A nurse had her arm wrapped around my mother, crying along with her. Later, Mom told us she saw the angels come and carry my father away to heaven. As my family left the hospital room, I walked back over to the bed where my father's body lay so still. I trembled when I touched his arm, fighting back the tears. As if he could hear me, I leaned over and said, "Good-bye, Dad."

Mom and I walked outside to the parking lot, and I turned back and looked at the hospital building. All I could think of was: *What do I do now?* For eight weeks, our life revolved around watching Dad struggle with cancer here at this hospital. Now that his battle was over, I felt so lost, like my story had ended. My mind couldn't yet comprehend that my dad had a new body, and he no longer walked with a limp. He was free from pain and free from cancer. He was now living forever with his Savior in his eternal, heavenly home.

While many people were celebrating Labor Day on Monday, the day after my father died, my family was preparing to meet friends and relatives at the funeral home. Walking over to the wooden casket, I looked down at my father's lifeless form. He had suffered so much that his body was skeletal. Less than two years prior, my father had walked me down the aisle on my wedding day. Now I found myself gazing down at the still shell of a man dressed in the same blue pinstripe suit that he wore at my marriage celebration. Cupping my hand, I gently reached inside the casket, touching the one who taught me about Jesus, and softly whispered, "Daddy."

Many people came to offer their condolences at the funeral home. Jerome Zehr was well respected and loved by those in our community. The funeral was held on Wednesday, September 5th. Our family filed in to the front of the church and sat down. I felt as though my mind was in a fog, and everything seemed to happen in slow motion. At the close of the service, the congregation sang an old familiar hymn:

Lift Your Glad Voices

Lift your glad voices in triumph on high,
For Jesus hath risen, and man shall not die.
Vain were the terrors that gathered around Him,
And short the dominion of death and the grave;
He burst from the fetters of darkness that bound Him,
Resplendent in glory to live and to save!
Loud was the chorus of angels on high,
"The Savior hath risen, and man shall not die."
Glory to God, in full anthems of joy;
The being He gave us death cannot destroy.

Sad were the life we must part with tomorrow,
If tears were our birthright, and death were our end;
But Jesus hath cheered the dark valley of sorrow,
And bade us, immortal, to Heaven ascend.
Lift then your voices in triumph on high,
"For Jesus hath risen, and man shall not die."

Public Domain, Henry Ware, Jr.

The harmony of four-part a capella singing soared to the rafters, lifting my spirits. The hope described in the words of this hymn brought a calm over my soul. Death does not have the final word!

At the gravesite, it was difficult to watch my father's body being lowered into the grave. It made everything about Dad's death so final. And yet, I knew it was only his physical shell. My earthly father was not there. My dad claimed the promise found in 2 Timothy: "I have fought the good fight, I have finished the race, I have kept the faith. Now there is in store for me the crown of righteousness, which the Lord, the righteous Judge, will award to me on that day – and not only to me, but also to all who have longed for his appearing" (2 Timothy 4:7-8).

A few weeks after the funeral, I was alone in the living room of our new home as grief came flooding over me. I was missing my dad so much, and a swarm of questions and thoughts came pouring out from my innermost being. *Why, God,* I thought, *did my dad have to suffer so much? Why did my dad have to die when he was so young? Dad will never know retirement and have opportunities to enjoy other things in life. Myron barely had a chance to know this wonderful man. I'm a newlywed and still need my dad!* I was still working through the trauma of my abuse, and now losing my dad was just another blow. *God, life is so unfair,* I thought. This piece of my life's puzzle was just too hard. I was convinced that I couldn't bear the weight of this loss.

Suddenly, I was nearly shaken from my seat as I heard God clearly speak to me by piercing my heart with these words: "Be still and know that I am God" (Psalm 46:10). To be still literally means "to cease striving, let it go." This truth from God's Word finally sunk in as I sobbed and realized that God will always be in control, no matter the circumstances. Daddies will get sick and die, but God is still God! Nothing will ever change the fact that He is God, our Creator, who loves us with an everlasting love! He can be trusted even with our deepest pain. Like my earthly father, I can trust my Heavenly Father's every word!

In the days leading up to the funeral, I wrote a poem in memory of my father that was read by one of the officiating pastors at the service. Over the next few weeks, I would lie in bed at night and recite the words to myself as a way of comfort. God gave me a melody, and the words became a song.

Tribute to Dad

When I was just a little girl, so small yet growing strong,
You told me Jesus loved me, and taught me right from wrong.
Your hand was there for me to hold as we would cross the street.
I knew I did not need to fear, for you were there with me.

Thank you, Lord, for giving me the best dad in the world.
Thanks for all those years I spent being Daddy's little girl.
He's gone now, and my life's been changed,
But he's in heaven with You, singing with the angels
Somewhere beyond the blue.

The years passed by so swiftly, and even if I'm now grown,
I've always been secure in the love that you have shown.
One day God told our family there would be a change of plans.
He allowed you to become very ill, and we did not understand.
For six long months you suffered, I stood there by your side.
You once again reached out your hand, as I safely placed it in mine.
I silently pleaded with the Lord, not wanting to let you go.
Desperately I held on tight, "Daddy, I'll miss you so!"

Ever gently our Heavenly Father helped me to release my grasp.
He slowly reached out His own hand for you to hold at last.
God be with you, Daddy Dear; rest quietly in His care.
Someday soon I, too, will be in heaven with you there!

Thank you, Lord, for giving me the best dad in the world!
Thanks for all those years I spent being Daddy's little girl!
He's gone now, and my life's been changed,
But he's in heaven with You, singing with the angels,
Somewhere beyond the blue.

Copyright © 1990 Judy Borntrager

5
THE BRIGHT PIECES: NEW BEGINNINGS

"For it is by grace you have been saved, through faith—and this is not from yourselves, it is the gift of God." (Ephesians 2:8)

M Y FATHER'S DEATH changed life for all of us, and my family had to find a new normal. Grief hit me in the most unexpected places.

A couple of months after my dad's funeral, the Christmas season was upon us. Myron and I were shopping in a local store, and I couldn't help but notice the Christmas decorations adorning the aisles. The bright lights and tinsel-covered Christmas trees, however, did little to lift my spirits. I stopped at the card rack to pick out some Christmas cards for family and friends. As I glanced through the cards, I suddenly noticed the ones specifically labeled, *"For Mom and Dad,"* and I immediately burst into tears. There I stood, sobbing loudly in the store, staring at all the pretty cards, and I realized I would never again buy a Christmas card that read: *"For Mom and Dad."* My hand flew up and covered my mouth in an attempt to stifle the sobs that would not stop. I knew from then on, my new normal would be buying a Christmas card that read: *"For Mom"* only. The pain was real and hurt deeply. It wasn't that I didn't love my mom or wasn't grateful she was still with us; rather, the pain came from the realization that my dad was gone, never to celebrate Christmas with us again.

Two months after my father's cancer diagnosis, my grandmother was diagnosed with lung cancer. Her cry of "Why can't it be me?" in the hospital hallway when we learned about Dad's cancer, had come to a harsh reality for her and for our family. Once again, I watched someone I dearly love fade away from the brutal harshness of this dreadful disease. Visiting my grandma in her home, I walked over to her bed and put my hand on her shoulder. I felt her skin and bones and shuddered. I recognized that this was just how my dad's shoulder felt when he had cancer and was so thin. Cancer was winning again, and I felt so distraught. My grandmother passed away six months after my father's death. At her gravesite, surrounded by family and relatives, I turned to my cousin standing next to me and cried, "It's too soon." I wasn't prepared for more change and grief in my life.

Over the next few months, my sadness slowly turned into acceptance as I first dealt with the loss of my father and then the loss of my grandmother. I began to embrace this new chapter, knowing that I always had my Heavenly Father who cared for me with His unconditional love. In addition to these life changes, Myron and I began a passage seeking new beginnings.

Leaving Tradition for Truth

Throughout the course of my father's and my grandmother's deaths, Myron and I were still in counseling seeking wholeness from the pain and hurt of our past. We continued to attend the conservative Mennonite church, but we were both growing restless and weary of a life of restrictions. As we grew in our knowledge of Scripture, we came to understand that our faith in Jesus has nothing to do with works of the flesh. I started to recognize that my own futile attempts at pleasing God by only wearing dresses, never cutting my hair, and wearing it up in a bun every day were robbing me of true joy and freedom.

In essence, I was telling God, "Yes, Jesus, I accept You as my Savior, but I need to dress and look a certain way in order for me to get to heaven." In other words, I was rejecting Jesus's death on the cross as punishment for my sins as being enough. For years, I had an unfounded fear that God would send me straight to hell if I deviated slightly to the left or to the right from what the conservative church taught if I didn't look and dress by certain standards. I was foolishly trusting in my own works so that God would be happy with me.

I am so thankful for the Christian home I was raised in and for my upbringing. I place no blame on my parents who were living out their faith in the way they were raised. There has never been any doubt of my parents' love for me and my siblings. But my eyes were opened as I began to fully comprehend the simple truth of God's Word.

I read the Apostle Paul's words in Philippians in a new light:

> But whatever were gains to me I now consider loss for the sake of Christ. What is more, I consider everything a loss because of the surpassing worth of knowing Christ Jesus my Lord, for whose sake I have lost all things. I consider them garbage, that I may gain Christ and be found in him, not having a righteousness of my own that comes from the law, but that which is through faith in Christ—the righteousness that comes from God on the basis of faith (Philippians 3:7-9).

Growing up, I knew I looked different from most people and often felt looked down upon. It was so freeing for me to realize that through Christ, we're forgiven and live by grace, not by the law, and that I needed to look to Jesus as the Author of my salvation. Something within me came alive when I finally understood that there is nothing we can do to earn our salvation. I was endeavoring to place the piece of legalism into the puzzle of my life. Satan loved to steal my joy with a burdensome list of dos and don'ts, and I eventually came to understand this as false teaching. Instead of forcing the piece of legalism to fit, it was a puzzle piece I needed to let go of because God did not intend this to be a part of my life. I embraced Romans 8: "Therefore, there is now no condemnation for those who are in Christ Jesus, because through Christ Jesus the law of the Spirit who gives life has set you free from the law of sin and death" (Romans 8:1-2).

Nothing I do or don't do will make God love me any less. His love is for me is so pure and so rich that I cannot do anything to earn it. The more I grasp this truth, the more I bask in the freedom of God's love and know that in Christ I am not condemned!

It took an unbelievable amount of courage for Myron and me to step away from our conservative roots and to start attending a new church. I remember how vulnerable and exposed I felt when I first began to wear blue jeans in public. Yet, I was no longer gripped by the chains of bondage and fear that God would punish me for dressing this way. Myron and I found a new freedom in learning to walk in the Spirit, and there was a peace and contentment we hadn't known before.

It's a Wedding!

For the first five years after Dad died, I watched my mother struggle with the hardship of being a widow. My siblings and I were all married, so Mom was alone, living in the family home in Topeka. I tried to support her as much as possible but knew I couldn't fully comprehend or understand the pain of her own grief.

As my mother maintained the family home on her own, my siblings and I spent time at the house sorting through a lot of Dad's things. Eventually, Mom came to the conclusion that taking care of the white house we called home for so many years was too much of a burden for her. A public personal property auction was held, selling many of my father's collectibles. Then we put our childhood home up for sale. It was difficult to let go. Countless memories that I will never forget were a part of that house.

In April 1994, Mom bought a house in another town located west of Topeka and moved in. It was a smaller home and yard, which made it much easier for Mom to take care of. My siblings and I assumed that this move would create a new normal for our mother and that life would continue in this way. At least that was my assumption, until the day I stopped by Mom's new home to visit. Mom was all smiles and even a little giddy as she said, "I had a date last night!" My mind was full of questions as I thought, *What? Who? When? Where?*

The biggest surprise to this new turn of events was with whom my mother had a date! Mom had a date with a man named Wilbur Miller. My father's first cousin, Wilbur is also the father of Ken Miller, who served on the Gospel Echoes Team Prison Ministry with me. Three months after my father died, Ken's mother was killed in an accident in Florida. I had grieved Ken's loss with him and his family.

Mom and Wilbur could not contain their joy as they continued to date and fall in love. It did my heart good to see them so happy together. It came as no surprise when only a few months later, Mom and Wilbur announced their engagement!

The wedding took place in the fall at the church where Mom attended, the same church where Myron and I met just eight years earlier. It was a simple but beautiful wedding. Myron and I were privileged to walk my mother down the aisle to meet her groom. Standing with Mom in the back of the church, waiting to begin the procession, I looked over at her and said, "Are you ready, Mom? You're going to be a wife again!" Her smile was radiant through her tears. Both of our families came together in celebration, and it was an honor to sing with Ken during the ceremony. Wilbur has four children, and since we are related as second cousins to each other, it made becoming a blended family much easier for all of us.

My mother only lived in her new home one and a half years. After she got married, that house was sold, and she moved 10 miles away into Wilbur's home where they began their new life together.

When Ken and I served on the prison ministry team, we never imagined the plans God had in store for us years later. I have a photo of all four of our parents that I dearly cherish, which was taken years earlier. They're sitting in front of a fireplace at a Christmas gathering in Florida when they were there celebrating the holidays with our team. That picture is a constant reminder of how God brought this piece of my life's puzzle together. It amazes me how God has a place for every piece of joy and pain in our life.

At the writing of this book, my mother and Wilbur will celebrate 24 years of marriage. While I miss my dad every day, I cannot fathom my life or my family's life without Wilbur being a part of it. God's plans are beyond my wildest comprehension. I have learned, and continue to learn, to trust in my Heavenly Father, who always knows best.

Darcy

A few years after Myron and I left the conservative church, we began attending a new church in Nappanee, Indiana. We were eager to keep learning and growing in our walk with Jesus, and we looked for ways to get involved and be a part of this church. I joined the church choir and worship team, and both Myron and I became a part of an active Sunday School class. One Sunday morning, there was an announcement in the church bulletin describing a Christian cancer support ministry that works with cancer patients and their families. They had a need for volunteers, which caught my interest, and I wanted to learn more about it.

Before my father's diagnosis, my first encounter with cancer was back in the 1970s when my uncle had leukemia. Our family went to the hospital to visit him, and as a young girl, I was alarmed at what I saw. I didn't even recognize him. Since then, three uncles, my grandmother, and my father all lost their lives to this horrible disease. Knowing firsthand the devastation of cancer, I wanted to become a part of this ministry. Once I joined the team as a volunteer, I was assigned a cancer patient. My role was to be a support to the patient and to their families, walking alongside them, showing them the love of Jesus as they walk the journey of cancer.

It was only by God's incredible design that I learned that the first patient assigned to me was Darcy, my blind friend from high school! Not only had she been diagnosed with cancer, but it was pancreatic cancer, the same cancer that took my dad's life. Since we had lost contact with each other after graduation, I often wondered what had happened to her. Darcy never married but was living in a city not too far from our home. My heart was saddened and shocked to learn of Darcy's cancer, but I was thankful for the opportunity to become a part of her life once again.

My first visit to see Darcy was so precious. She was a patient at a local hospital, and I walked into her room, poked my head around the corner and said, "Darcy, it's Judy." She immediately lifted up her head and held out her arms. I walked over to her bed, where we enveloped each other in a gigantic hug! It had been more than 20 years since I last had seen her, and Darcy still looked the same from our days in high school, with her beautiful brown hair and bright smile that lit up a room. That day was the beginning of a renewed friendship for us!

Over the next few months, I went to visit Darcy often at the apartment where she lived. I tagged along with her and her family to doctor appointments or out to lunch together. I treasured these moments of being able to minister to Darcy in this way. I loved the sweet times of just being with her. Darcy especially enjoyed it when I read to her. At other times, we would sit outside on her swing drinking lemonade, talking about our days in school or about heaven and eternity. Sometimes we cried together. I knew Darcy went to church as a child, and she could sing all the children's songs that were sung in Sunday School, but I wasn't sure if she attended church as an adult. Darcy was dying, and the more time I spent with her, the more I wanted to share with her the joy and security my faith in Jesus gave me.

On July 30, 2002, Darcy and I were in her living room talking about heaven. The conversation turned to the topic of eternal life, and I asked her if she wanted to ask Jesus into her heart. I wanted to leap and shout a loud cry of "Hallelujah" when she nodded her head yes! There in the quietness of her home, we bowed our heads in prayer. Darcy asked Jesus to forgive her of her sins and for Him to live in her heart as her Lord and Savior, just as I had done so many years ago. In the book of John, it says, "Yet to all who did receive him, to those who believed in his name, he gave the right to become children of God" (John 1:12). My heart rejoiced as I knew my beloved friend was now my sister in Christ!

By September, Darcy's cancer had progressed. During one Sunday evening visit, Darcy seemed more restless than usual. I plopped myself down next to her on the bed and asked, "Darcy, do you want me to sing?" I had to laugh as she shook her head no. Taking her hand anyway, I started to sing "Jesus Loves Me." I noticed a calmness come over her as she lay back on her pillow and closed her eyes. Darcy began to mouth every word right along with me as she fell into a peaceful sleep. I left her home that evening with a heavy heart, wondering if this would be the last time I would see her. It turned out to be so. Three days later, Darcy took the hand of Jesus as He led her to her eternal home. Upon hearing of Darcy's death, my heart ached, but I cherished that last sweet memory I had of singing with her.

Prior to her death, Darcy had asked me to sing at her funeral, and the family asked that I give the eulogy. It was extremely difficult to get through, but participating in the service was a gift and a way for me to give something to Darcy's family, who had come to mean so much to me. A couple of weeks later, I received a thank-you card in the mail from her family. Tears welled up inside me. Tucked inside the card was a beautiful necklace with a gold pendant of an angel, along with a hand-written note from Darcy's mother. That necklace is so precious to me and is a constant reminder of my friendship with Darcy.

I'm confident it wasn't simply a coincidence that I met Darcy all those years ago back in the seventh grade. It was all part of God's perfect plan, just like all the various pieces of my life's puzzle. This puzzle piece gave me some answers to the question of *why*. I now understand that because of my father's battle with cancer and eventual death, I was able to re-enter Darcy's life and share the good news of eternal salvation with her, and I know there is at least one soul in heaven because of it! That makes the pain of losing Dad easier. Who am I to question God's ways? I'm learning that perhaps God knows what He's doing after all!

PHOTOGRAPHS

Jerome and Mary Waneta Zehr, my mother and father,
on their Wedding Day in 1956

Judy with the curl on top of her head on her fourth birthday

Judy, at age 5, playing the antique player piano that is now in her home

Dad's store in Topeka, Indiana

The old Topeka Fire Station that was located
next to my dad's store
(These buildings have since been torn down.)

Mom working in her flower garden
with the large swing in the background

Mom and Dad in our Topeka, Indiana, childhood home

Judy playing piano and singing with the Gospel Echoes Team

Mr. & Mrs. Myron Borntrager.
Our Wedding Day in 1988

Building our new home

Mom and Dad after Dad's cancer diagnosis

Mom and Dad as Parade Marshals
for the Topeka Fourth of July parade in 1990

Mom and Dad riding in the red convertible as Parade Marshals

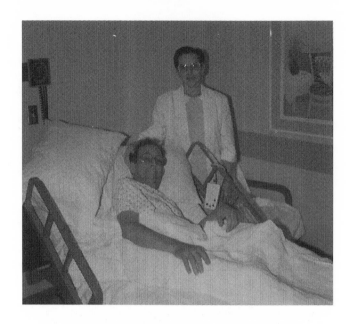

Mom at the hospital with Dad

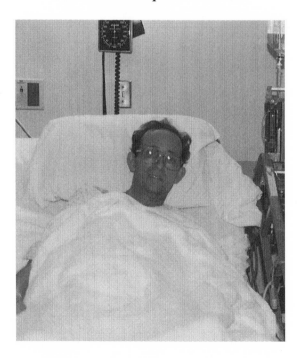

My father's last days in the hospital

Photographs

Mom and Wilbur's Wedding Day

Mom and Wilbur

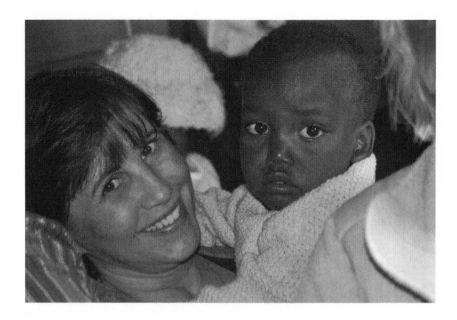

Judy with her little orphan friend in Africa

Judy's friend enjoying his peanut butter sandwich

Judy in Africa with her buddy MoMo

Myron holding Precious Angel at the Africa Gospel Church Baby Centre

Darcy

*Myron and Judy during
their 25th wedding anniversary celebration*

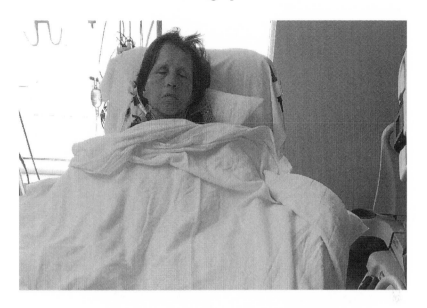

Judy in the ICU after open heart surgery

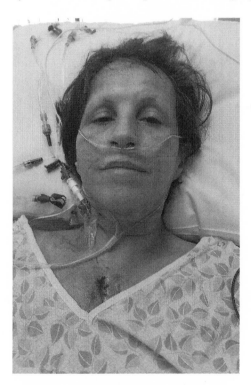

Judy following her heart surgery

Judy performing on stage at Heritage Hall
(Photo by Das Dutchman Essenhaus. Used by Permission.)

Myron and Judy

6
THE HIDDEN PIECES:
JOURNEY OF PAIN

"I will instruct you and teach you in the way you should go; I will counsel you with my loving eye on you." (Psalm 32:8)

I T IS OFTEN difficult to know how the hard pieces of your life can fit together. The first years of our marriage were filled with pain and heartache. Married fewer than five years, we began to build our new house while confronting the sting of my past sexual abuse and Myron's painful issues of rejection. Then we watched my father, followed by my grandmother, die of cancer. It was beyond tough. The one bright spot of joy during this time was my mother getting married again and walking her down the aisle. I had hoped for more bright spots in Myron's and my future, but three weeks after my mom's wedding, I underwent a surgery that left me feeling lost and emotionally empty.

A Life-Altering Choice

Unlike most little girls, when I was young and growing up, it wasn't a daydream of mine to one day get married and have children. Rather than play with dolls, I was much more content to ride my bike through the neighborhood, swing on our large swing in the backyard, hang upside-down on monkey bars, race around with my brother in his go-kart, and climb things like trees or picnic tables (and break my arm)! My mother's older sister never got married, and I often spoke of being just like this aunt, declaring that when she grew old, I was going to move in with her and become her caretaker! It's amusing how a person changes their mind in the course of their lifetime. That longing and dream of marriage and children came years later for me. Fast-forward

40-plus years. At the writing of this book, my aunt still lives by herself, she is over 90 years old, and I am a married woman!

During our engagement, Myron and I talked of having either two or three children. Myron longed for a little girl, and I imagined our daughter having luscious brown curls (like her father) that would bounce in the wind. After we were married, our plans were suddenly thrown a curveball when I underwent some medical tests for pain I was experiencing. The tests revealed an alarming deformity related to my kidneys. "No wonder you're having pain," my doctor exclaimed. We were all surprised to discover that these two bean-shaped organs of mine were not located where they were supposed to be and were joined together and pressing on other organs, which likely was the cause of my pain. While the kidneys were functioning normally, we were told this deformity could potentially cause some health concerns for me, should I become pregnant. More than one doctor confirmed I would be considered a high-risk pregnancy. Learning of this abnormality was a shock to us, and I wasn't sure how to process the news.

Several doctor visits later, I sat in the office of a nephrologist, a kidney specialist, at IU Medical Center in Indianapolis. My kidneys were functioning; therefore, no surgery was needed to correct the deformity. However, because of their odd position and being fused together, the doctor explained it was like living with one kidney. This kidney defect, along with other health complications I was dealing with at the time, left me in a dangerous situation. The specialist was frank with me. Peering through his glasses, he looked me in the eye and was straightforward as he said, "You have to make a decision—and soon." Meaning, either I get pregnant now with the high risks involved or decide to never become pregnant. I had a choice to make, and at age 33, it was a choice I had never anticipated.

A few weeks went by as I wrestled with my thoughts and desperately prayed for God's guidance, begging Him to please give me an answer! I felt so torn and confused. Ultimately, it had to be a decision only Myron and I could make together. It was agonizing and the most difficult decision of my life when I reluctantly made an appointment with my gynecologist. He agreed to perform the surgery of an irreversible tubal ligation.

After the surgery, my physical recovery was quick. The emotional part, however, was a completely different story. My mother's heart was empty and wounded. The realization that I would never be able to physically carry a child in my womb left a deep sadness within me. It took little to trigger my emotions of grief and loss. Catching a glimpse of a baby's face staring back at me from the pages of a magazine caused an eruption of anguished tears. I grieved the loss, knowing I would never know what my child would have looked like. There were days when I was riddled with guilt and shame. My thoughts tormented me. *Did Myron and I not trust the Lord enough to bring me through a high-risk pregnancy? Did we make a mistake? Was this truly the right decision?* I questioned. My doctor assured me my emotions were quite normal as I faced the enormity of it all. Yet, this reality was another hard blow in my life's puzzle—and a piece I had never foreseen.

Following my surgery, everything was too fresh for Myron and me to even think about adoption. When we talked about having children, we believed that to mean holding our own flesh and blood in our arms. Years later, there were further health issues for me, and it became clear that even if I never had had a tubal ligation, it was uncertain if I could have ever become pregnant. There were just too many complications with my body. At the age of 46, I had a complete abdominal hysterectomy, and because of the strange placement of my kidneys, this was a delicate surgery. Special medical testing was done prior to the surgery, and I recall my surgeon being very honest with me. "You're a hard case," she said. "If I make one wrong snip, I'll destroy your kidney function," she explained. Many prayers were said for me, and God was ever so faithful in guiding the doctor's hands. He answered every prayer that was said on my behalf when I came through the surgery without any complications.

The fact remains, Myron and I made the right decision for me to never become pregnant. Yet, in spite of knowing this, I still struggled with the pain and heartache of it all.

Without talking to anyone about my pain, I took this very difficult piece in the puzzle of my life and neatly tucked it away in a box, putting it up high on a shelf. In bold letters, the box read *FAILURE*, which only added fuel to my pain. I labeled myself a failure because I would never experience pregnancy and childbirth, which I deemed to be the ultimate achievement for a woman. I understand that people mean well when they ask, "Do you and your husband have children?" But the sting it brings to my heart is real. I usually manage a weak smile and answer with a simple "No." I never talked about the box. I just left it there in the closet and walked away. Over the years, bit by bit, God revealed some startling truths to me that finally helped to bring closure.

7
THE MEANINGFUL PIECES: BLESSINGS IN DISGUISE

"The Spirit you received does not make you slaves, so that you live in fear again; rather, the Spirit you received brought about your adoption to sonship. And by him we cry, 'Abba, Father.'" (Romans 8:15)

HAVING NO CHILDREN in our home gave Myron and me greater opportunities to travel, and we began participating in mission trips. Two unforgettable trips involved us working in orphanages, filling a deep longing within my heart. Working with teams from our church, we traveled to Quito, Ecuador, and a few years later, we flew to Kenya, Africa.

When we first stepped foot inside the orphanage in Quito, I met an energetic little girl named Rita. With her big brown eyes and dark brown hair all tied up in ponytails, Rita showed no signs of bashfulness as she marched right up to me and grabbed my hand. My heart melted like a puddle of butter! Taking care of both toddlers and babies, our days were filled with changing diapers, reading stories, and helping at lunchtime. My mothering instincts kicked in, and my spirit was filled to overflowing. There were cute giggles and laughter while teaching the children motions to the old favorite song "Patty Cake" as we sat around the lunchroom table. The children's curiosity and wide-eyed wonder when learning new things were priceless.

One day, our team drove to another orphanage about an hour's drive outside of Quito. At this particular orphanage, I was drawn to a precious three-month-old infant who instantly stole my heart. Baby Darnell was so snuggly and soft as I held him close and bottle-fed him. My mother's heart was full and content. I held him all day, and my arms never grew tired or weary as I kept looking into the eyes of this tiny bundle of happiness. Amazingly, Baby Darnell never cried and barely made a sound. He just kept gazing back at me with his big beautiful eyes.

When the time came for our team to depart and make the trip back to Quito, I was not ready to go. Climbing the stairs clutching Baby Darnell tightly in my arms, I felt my heart literally being torn in two as I walked into his room. I carefully laid him down in his crib and took one last look at that sweet face. With a deep ache in my heart, I turned and walked away, knowing I would never see Baby Darnell again. *What was going to happen to him?* I wondered. *What kind of life was Baby Darnell facing?* Before I could stop myself, I blurted out to Myron that I longed to adopt Baby Darnell. We both were aware, however, that adoptions outside the country of Ecuador are extremely rare. Although we talked briefly of adoption in the past, we truthfully never felt God's leading in that direction. That day in Ecuador was the closest I ever came in wanting to adopt. We both agreed and felt confident that this was not God's chosen path for us, and we were at peace with that decision. I am grateful for the moments I had with each precious child I met in Ecuador, never to be forgotten.

Mathare Slums of Nairobi

Myron and I flew to Kenya in 2009, and our team's first stop was the slums of Nairobi. It had recently rained, so the van was unable to descend the muddy ravine to our destination, and it was not safe for us to walk. Leaving the van at the top of the hill, we rode down the slippery, murky slope in a four-wheel-drive Land Rover. Staring at the unthinkable, we were astonished at the conditions in which people lived. Dressed in tattered clothes, individuals sat outside their shacks and huts with looks of despair and hopelessness. A child was pulling a makeshift toy made from a two-liter soda bottle, using bottle caps for wheels and wire as axles. It's impossible to put into words what we witnessed. "Oh God," I silently cried, "have mercy on these poor souls!"

The Meaningful Pieces: Blessings in Disguise

The truck came to a halt as it pulled in front of the orphanage we were visiting. We were told children in this home ranged in age from three years old up to age 15. In spite of their meager and stark surroundings, the children's joy was infectious as they eagerly lined up outside and sang a song for us with gusto and delight! Then our team passed out half of a peanut butter sandwich, one small box of crayons, and one coloring page to each child while one by one, they waited patiently for their turn. The children were ecstatic and immediately began to color and eat their sandwiches! The director of this ministry to the orphans explained that for many of these children, this was their only meal of the day. The peanut butter was a vital source of protein for them. We watched several of the children take a bite and then slip the remainder of the sandwich into their pocket. It was unknown if they were saving it for later or to share with someone else, perhaps a sibling. We gave so little, but their faces told the story. The children's cheerful demeanor had a great impact on all of us.

While still outside, it began to rain, making the slums extremely muddy. We quickly had to move our team and the children inside to a very small room to present the devotions we planned to share. While standing shoulder-to-shoulder in these tight quarters, another team member nudged me and said, "Judy, I think he needs a friend!" I looked down into the face of a little boy with tears streaming down his cheeks and arms raised up to me! I immediately picked him up, and without hesitation, he threw his arms around my neck and held on so tight as if to say, "Don't ever let me go!" Pressing his face next to mine, I held him for a very long time as he fell asleep in my arms. God showed up in unexpected ways that day as He showed me that these orphans long for love and comfort just like any other child.

The rain eventually stopped, and we moved back outside. My new little friend began to wake up and then accidently peed on me! I laughed as I put him down and watched him dash away! It was healing for me to hold a child who needed love and comfort, filling a need once again in my mother's heart.

Our team left the slums with a three-hour drive ahead of us as we headed to the Africa Gospel Church Baby Centre. Traveling the rough, bumpy terrain, I could not forget that little face peering up at me. From that experience, while riding in the van, a song was born—the words etched only in my head and heart until I later arrived at the Baby Centre and could finally write it all down.

God's Love Came

In the slums of Africa, I looked into his eyes,
And saw those precious tears, little arms stretched up to mine.
Reaching down, I picked him up, tiny hands around my neck
Just wanting to be loved, his head upon my chest.
Never the same, no never the same.
Forever my life's changed, I knew that God's love came,
The day I held an orphan in my arms.
God's plan so unexpected on that day!
Cause in those eyes I left my heart, left my heart to stay!
Never the same, no never the same,
Forever my life's changed, I knew that God's love came,
The day I held an orphan in my arms!

Copyright © 2009 Judy Borntrager

Africa Gospel Church Baby Centre

The Africa Gospel Church Baby Centre, located in Ngata, Kenya, is a beautiful and amazing place. Our church in Nappanee, Indiana, partnered with the Africa Gospel Church to build this orphanage. Many orphans have been adopted and placed in their forever homes.

While working at the Baby Centre, three-year-old MoMo captured my heart! His bright smile and spirit were contagious. Even though there was a language barrier between us, God communicated through the heart of this child! As I walked past each crib with an infant in it, I would ask MoMo, "What's his/her name?" MoMo didn't speak English very well, but he understood what I was asking and promptly blurted out each baby's name!

Just like our experience in Ecuador, I embraced our days of loving babies and toddlers at the Baby Centre. I took MoMo to the learning center room where we worked with cardboard bricks, stacking them as tall as we could while naming the color of each brick. MoMo's laughter and energy grew on me. He was so eager to learn! In between stacking the bricks, I kept running after another toddler, Malachi, who was fascinated with the bathroom toilets, splashing in them and spilling the water all over the floor!

Another unforgettable day at the Baby Centre was when our team dressed up the toddlers for a photo shoot for the Baby Centre's annual Christmas card. The toddlers were dressed as angels, shepherds, Mary and Joseph, and even little sheep. I helped MoMo change into the Joseph costume, asking him to take his shirt off. MoMo could hardly contain his excitement, and before I could stop him, he had stripped himself naked! I eventually managed to get MoMo's pants back on, and our team succeeded in getting all the rambunctious toddlers to pose flawlessly! MoMo was truly the star and a perfect Joseph for this nativity scene!

MoMo became my special buddy as I formed a close bond with him. He blew me kisses, and I blew them right back! In his broken English, he would say, "I love you vardy, vardy mooch!" Whether it was playing hide-and-seek or pushing him on the swing where I told him he was flying to the moon, I cherished each moment I had with him because I knew these moments would all too soon come to an end.

I loved watching Myron interact with the children at this orphanage. I observed a softer side to him that I had never seen before. After one particularly hard day of work projects around the building, Myron was exhausted, and he sat down on the ground outside to take a break. Little Precious Angel (her actual name) quickly came over to him and crawled right into his lap and laid her head down on his chest. I noticed complete contentment on both of their faces. It was a priceless moment and a scene that is forever etched in my memory.

During one of our final evenings at the Baby Centre, our team was invited to the home of the pastor of the Africa Gospel Church. It was a memorable time of eating a meal together and sharing life experiences with each other. As we shared our stories, the pastor was greatly impacted by Myron's and my story of never having a child of our own. He asked both of us to kneel on the floor in the living room while his family and the rest of the mission team gathered around us. Laying hands on us, the pastor prayed a special prayer of blessing over Myron and me. We were so moved by his love and compassion. The team began to sing songs of praise, and I could not stop the tears that were spilling down my face. For the first time, I felt someone's genuine care and concern over our being childless, and there was great healing for my soul.

When the day came for our team to leave the Baby Centre, I didn't want to leave this beautiful piece of heaven. My last memory is walking through the gate to the backyard and closing it behind me. I leaned over the fence and looked at the faces of children I had grown to love. I spotted MoMo staring back at me, fingers in his mouth. My heart was breaking for him and for me. I didn't want to abandon this precious child. Refusing to let MoMo see me cry, I fought back the tears and said, "I love you very much, MoMo!" Once again, my mind was filled with *What is going to happen to MoMo?* I turned and walked away, letting the tears flow freely as they trickled down my face. I was relieved to learn that a few months later, MoMo was adopted by his forever family.

Our team gathered out front praying and singing praises to God for all He had done on this mission trip. I left a piece of my heart at the Africa Gospel Church Baby Centre. God met me there, and my cup was overflowing with gratitude.

Closure

It took me many years, but I finally went back to the closet where I had hidden the box labeled *FAILURE*. Reaching up, I carefully brought the box down from the shelf. With trembling hands, I opened it up and stared that painful puzzle piece right in the face. "It's time," God said. "It's time to rename the box." Guiding my hand, God helped me scratch out the ugly word *FAILURE* and had me replace it with *DAUGHTER.*

"You're my child," I heard Him say. "You're a daughter of the King, and you are not a failure," God said. "Really?" I asked. "I am not a failure?" Looking up to the heavens, I breathed in hope and let out a sigh. "Thank you, Lord," I cried! I felt a freedom I hadn't felt in a long time.

I will never be a mother. I will never hear the words "Grandma" calling me from the lips of a child. And yet, God has given me nieces and nephews that I love dearly and have helped care for in their growing-up years. They have become my "kids." And working with orphans has given me an opportunity to love children who are in desperate need. I am thankful for God's presence and healing in each of these moments.

Miraculous Healing

One of the greatest miracles of healing in my life came during a 2008 mission trip to Mexico. Led by one of the pastors from our church, our mission team was part of a prayer walk. We worked with churches in the greater Juarez, Mexico, area, going into homes, sharing meals together, and praying for any special needs these fellow brothers and sisters in Christ might have. We participated in several church services, and were so blessed and touched as fellow believers surrounded our team, praying over us! It made such an impact to see these people with so little giving us so much by their love and prayers!

During our time there, one of our stops was outside the home of a witch doctor. Maya, a Mexican church worker and partner in our ministry, informed our team that the lady living in this house was known for practicing witchcraft. We couldn't help but notice how this house stood out from other homes located in such a poor community, and we asked how this could be? Maya put it simply by explaining this house is larger and nicer because the witch doctor profits from her power. Standing in a circle, our team started to pray, when suddenly, music began blaring loudly from an outside speaker. The team kept praying, asking for God's power to be present and for the enemy, Satan, to be defeated. Just as suddenly as it began, the music stopped. We knew without a doubt that the Lord heard our prayers and intervened in a miraculous way.

Another stop took our team to a sand dune located outside the city. Gazing up at the large hill, Maya told us the story of witchcraft being practiced here with rape and murder being common occurrences. On every Halloween, witches gather at the peak of the sand dune and claim the land for Satan as far as they can see. Since this area is just across the Mexican border, a person can easily see over into the United States from the top of that hill. Our team could feel the heaviness and oppression that was in the air. It was a bright, sunny day, but I looked around and could feel nothing but darkness. As we stood in that desolate place, our answer was to pray the Name of Jesus over this land and to claim it back for the Lord!

One day, while sharing a meal together with one of the local church congregations, Maya pointed out a young boy to me. Jose, Maya said, was a child who at one time was so full of joy, but now the light was gone from his eyes. I gasped when Maya explained that Jose had been sexually abused and was no longer the same joyful little boy. I felt an immediate connection to this child who had become so broken. Maya walked over to Jose and began praying for him. I quickly followed and knelt down beside them both. Feeling young Jose's anguish and hurt, I recognized his look of pain. He sat there quietly staring at the floor. Since he did not speak English, I asked Maya if she could translate something to Jose for me. I began to cry as I said, "Tell him to never forget how much Jesus loves him!" Looking up, Jose reached over and gave me a hug. I have never forgotten this little boy; I can only pray that he has found healing that only comes from Jesus.

After one particularly long and tiring day, our team gathered together in our dorms and spent some time debriefing and sharing stories. After my experience of meeting Jose, I felt compelled to share my story of my past sexual abuse and God's healing in my life. As I shared, one of the Mexican church workers, a young girl named Elise, began to cry. She could not speak English, but she listened and understood my story through the words of an interpreter. As I finished, the interpreter asked, "So what do we do for Elise?" I didn't understand the question, but then the interpreter explained to us that Elise had also been sexually abused. My heart jumped a few beats, and I took a deep breath. Our pastor asked if I would take Elise to another room and pray with her. Getting up from the table, I took Elise, and Maya who could interpret, into a back bedroom. All three of us sat down on the beds as Elise began to spill out her story. Elise had never told anyone of her sexual abuse before, and she trembled as she recalled the horrific details, sharing them for the first time. With Maya interpreting, I listened and gasped with my eyes getting wider when I learned that Elise's story of sexual abuse was *identical* to mine, down to every detail! It had the same circumstances of how and where the abuse happened, and was the same family member who was the perpetrator.

I could feel Elise's pain become my pain as God miraculously allowed me to identify with her! We shared a long hug as I prayed with her. I held her face in my hands while I sang to her and wiped away the tears from her eyes. In that moment, I saw the good from that ugly, painful puzzle piece that tormented me for so very long, and it fit **perfectly**! I clearly saw God reach out His hand, take that piece, and make it a perfect fit in the puzzle of my life. God had been preparing me all along for this exact moment. It answered the question of *why* that I had asked so many times and for so many years.

God's timing is amazing, and His ways are always best. He was redeeming what I thought was something unredeemable. As I saw the pieces of my life start to fit together, I began to catch a glimpse of what I recognized to be a beautiful picture.

8

THE CORE PIECES: STRAIGHT TO THE HEART

"For you created my inmost being; you knit me together in my mother's womb. I praise you because I am fearfully and wonderfully made; your works are wonderful, I know that full well." (Psalm 139:13)

M YRON AND I celebrated 30 years of marriage in 2018. Through the years, with all the ups and downs of our life, God has been present, and incredible healing has taken place. While the journey has been difficult, the lessons we have learned are irreplaceable.

Before we were married, Myron lived in Phoenix, Arizona, for four years. He loved living in the Valley of the Sun, and it was always a dream of his to one day live there again. When he was offered a sales position with an HVAC company based in Montreal, Quebec, it gave him an opportunity to work out of a home office. We sought God's direction, and Myron took this job in 2013.

Seeking another new beginning, I left my office job of nearly 10 years, and in December of that year, we packed up our SUV, traveled across the country, and never looked back. At the writing of this book, we've already spent six winters living in Arizona; we return to Indiana during the summer months. We have fallen in love with our new church community, our neighbors, and the beauty of the desert. My love of music and singing compelled me to join our church choir and to participate in several different worship teams and singing ensembles. I also started doing volunteer work at the office of a local Christian organization.

The first couple of years we lived in the Southwest were a peaceful and happy time. I was grateful for God's goodness. However, my quiet, comfortable world was abruptly shattered when storm clouds moved in, and the waves tossed me like a ragdoll deep into the dark, uncharted waters of the sea.

A Scary Diagnosis

In 2017, while in Arizona, I had a routine wellness check with a general practitioner whose office was close to our area. After carefully listening to my heart with his stethoscope, the doctor said he heard a loud heart murmur. That did not alarm me, however, since I was born with a heart murmur, and throughout my life, I was never told by a doctor to seek further testing. Yet, this general practitioner was concerned enough about my condition that he referred me to a cardiologist.

My first visit to see the cardiologist was in March. I explained the symptoms I was experiencing, and the physician didn't seem too worried. He said, "It's probably a rhythm issue with your heart that can be controlled with medication. Let's get some testing done and go from there." Two days later I had an echocardiogram, followed by a four-week period of wearing a heart event monitor. While I hated wearing the bulky heart monitor 24 hours a day, seven days a week, I went about my daily duties, convinced there was no reason to be anxious.

Near the end of April, I returned to the cardiologist's office for a follow-up appointment. Sitting on the edge of the exam table with my legs dangling over the side, I was expecting to hear some good news. The doctor was calm and very matter-of-fact as he explained his findings. "You have aortic valve stenosis," he said. "Your valve is narrowed and weakened, and you have age-related calcification around the valve. You need to follow up in Indiana."

My legs stopped swinging, and I felt my body stiffen while I let out a silent gasp. His words slapped me hard in the face. Every fiber of my being was screaming and protesting a loud *no*!

I was already scheduled to perform in a show at Heritage Hall that summer, with rehearsals beginning soon, and this diagnosis would certainly interfere with those plans! (It did. Much to everyone's disappointment, I had to back out of performing that summer.) My head was in a fog and began to spin. I wanted to cry, stomp my feet, and kick something! I was too stunned to ask questions, even though my head was full of them. I went home in a daze.

Not Me!

About a week after my diagnosis, we returned to Indiana. Two days later, I met with my family doctor to see whom she recommended that I see for follow-up treatment. Watching her walk into the room, I couldn't help but notice that she wasn't her usual cheery self. There was a grim look on her face. The first words out of her mouth were, "What is going on? You need a new heart valve." Restricting my activities, including my favorite walks along the lake, my doctor referred me to a well-known cardiothoracic surgeon in our area.

Looking back, I realized I had experienced symptoms for nearly two years prior and had just ignored them. I first noticed symptoms while standing at my kitchen counter, and suddenly a dark cloud covered my eyes. My heart started flip-flopping and beating in a funny manner, and I nearly passed out. After a few seconds, the episode was over, and I felt fine. These episodes, however, continued. Then I became more aware of fatigue and shortness of breath. Walking uphill, climbing a flight of stairs, or even singing left me feeling winded and dizzy.

One day I spent several hours working outside on our landscaping. I wasn't quite finished pulling weeds and hauling debris in the wheelbarrow when suddenly I felt faint and very weak. My heart began doing funny things. I immediately sat down on the front porch steps. Seconds passed, and the episode didn't stop like all the other times. I panicked. Myron was not home, and my cell phone was inside the house. I saw two of my neighbors across the road in their driveway, but I was unable to call to them or to get up and walk to them. I just sat there wondering what would happen if I lost consciousness. I prayed they would notice me, but they never looked my way.

After what seemed like hours, the faintness slowly began to diminish. I stood up and thought I could put the gardening tools and wheelbarrow away and get into the house for a shower. I made it from the front porch to the back of the house when I immediately had to sit down again. I sat there and waited for what seemed like an eternity for the lightheadedness to pass. Finally, the episode was over, and I went into the house. But once again, I ignored the incident thinking it was a fluke and nothing serious. I carried on with life as usual until the day I heard those dreadful, terrifying words from the cardiologist. I couldn't ignore these symptoms any longer and finally realized how serious they were.

Just when I thought my puzzle was picture-perfect, I faced a situation I didn't think I could handle. I did not want any part of this puzzle piece in my life. I wanted to throw it far away. Other people could handle stuff like this. I had already had my life's share of hardship. Didn't God know I didn't want any more?

Praises of the Heart

Shortly after arriving back in Indiana, I was scheduled to sing a solo with our church choir during all three of our Sunday morning worship services. This song was going to require a lot of breath, power, and stamina. I was eager to sing it but secretly wondered how I would be able to sing such a difficult solo piece with my shortness of breath. I shared my recent diagnosis with the choir, and they were so supportive with their love and prayers. Despite my fears, God met my needs that morning. Through His power, I had the strength needed to sing in every service without any shortness of breath. God moved in each of us, and His timing of this song was so perfect! The message being sung was all about blessing the Lord. He showed me His power would meet all of the fears I had, even with the fresh news of my heart condition staring me in the face. God was telling me to simply praise Him through it all! He gave me every breath I needed that morning to sing His praise! Through tears of gratitude, I praised the Name of Jesus, my Provider.

The Heart of the Matter

I saw the cardiothoracic surgeon at the end of June. The surgeon came into the room, and before he even sat down, he said, "Your valve is a wreck." The only option was open heart surgery to replace my aortic valve. Without surgery, the doctor explained, my life expectancy was only about two years. He confirmed that I was born with this defective heart valve, describing that the aortic valve has three leaflets that open and close as it pumps blood throughout the body. When it's opened, the opening is about the size of a quarter. My eyes grew wide when the surgeon told us that two of the three leaflets in my valve were fused together and never opened. That left the opening of my aortic valve to roughly about the size of a straw. In addition, my valve had calcified with age, making the opening even smaller. I let out a sigh. We finally understood the cause of my heart murmur, and this diagnosis explained why I was nearly passing out.

Surgery was scheduled for a couple of weeks later, and until then, my activities continued to be greatly restricted. I was not allowed to exercise, and the doctor ordered me to act like an old lady! Contemplating what was ahead, Myron and I went home to wait.

During this waiting period, I looked back over my life. I remembered as a child how breathless I became when running around outside playing with the neighborhood kids, riding my bike, or mowing the lawn. There was the day I ran a race with my classmates around the school track during our physical education class. I came in last place and attributed it to being out of shape, when in fact, it was my defective heart valve. I couldn't help but wonder why God kept me alive all these years. Without realizing it at the time, our difficult decision for me to have tubal ligation surgery back in 1995 was God's divine protection over me. My kidney deformity, coupled with a defective heart value, meant childbirth may have been fatal for me, and we marvel at God's timely intervention. So many emotions left me feeling perplexed, and yet, I remained hopeful. In the midst of such uncertainty and fear, I chose to exercise my faith and to remain in the God who created me. I chose to trust the promises I found each day in His Word. I was not looking forward to another surgery, especially one that was going to be so difficult. But I knew God would come through as He always had before.

God reminded me that I was alive for a reason, even while growing up with a bad heart valve. I remembered how the Lord had met me through hardship and loss—death, abuse, broken dreams, and now, near-death experiences. I was drawn to God's promises found in Scripture. In the book of John, I read, "Out of his fullness we have all received grace in place of grace already given" (John 1:16). I've received many blessings over the years and knew without a doubt, I could trust my God during such a time as this.

July 13, 2017: Surgery Day

I lay on my hospital bed waiting to be taken back to surgery. Looking around the room, I saw my husband, Mom and Wilbur, my sister, a niece, my dear aunt, a precious friend, and one of our pastors from church surrounding me. The pastor prayed, and I experienced a peace in the room. I felt no fear in that moment because God's presence was so powerful. Then it was time. Hugs were shared, *I love yous* said, and I was wheeled down the hallway and into the operating room.

My mother wrote in my journal for me:

We are here! Thank you so much, Lord, for Your presence right here right now, with Judy and all of us as we wait...calm our hearts, Lord. Nurse Kendra just informed us that she is in surgery. Nurse Kendra came to update us again. She said they're at the place where they stop her heart...but we pray the doctor's hands are guided by the Lord. 12:45 and we're ready for the consultation with the doctor. Thank you, Lord! It's over! What a blessing. They put in a cow's valve instead of a pig's. The doctor said it's working beautifully. We're rejoicing! Well, finally we got to go see Judy and oh you hardly looked like yourself, it made us teary-eyed. They were trying to wake you up, but there were still tubes here and there, and they had you covered up from head to toe to keep you warm. Praise God, Praise God, Praise God!

I woke up in the ICU covered in a warm blanket. I was propped up in the bed because it was too painful to lay flat. My breastbone had been split open and was now held together with two titanium plates, wire, and eight screws. The nurses instructed me not use my arms to push or lift anything for six weeks until my breastbone healed. After only four days, I was released from the hospital, but recovery from this surgery was going to be a long, hard process.

Unexpected Complications

Two weeks after surgery I developed a cough, and there was a tightness in my chest. It was hard to breathe and difficult to talk. I was encouraged to walk as much as possible during my recovery but found it to be nearly intolerable. My follow-up appointment at the surgeon's office confirmed our fears when x-rays showed fluid in my lungs. We were told to not be concerned, however, because fluid in the lungs can happen after heart surgery. I returned to the hospital the following day and had one and one-half liters of fluid drained from my right lung. We hoped and prayed that this would be the solution and that no further trips to the hospital would be needed.

Nevertheless, over the next few weeks, this became a pattern for me in my recovery. We made repeated trips to the hospital to have fluid drained, always from my right lung. It was painful and exhausting and took me the rest of the day to recover. As fluid was drained, my lung would start to expand, causing a lot of pain, and I would begin to cough. At times, they would need to stop the procedure so I could catch my breath.

Seven weeks after surgery, I was still weak and not regaining my strength. I didn't feel good and had a hard time eating and sleeping. My right lung continued to fill with fluid. On my fourth visit to the hospital, the physician performing the thoracentesis consulted with my surgeon over the phone. During surgery, while on the heart and lung machine with my heart stopped, my lungs were collapsed. For reasons unknown, my right lung never fully expanded back to normal after surgery. Pockets developed in this lung where fluid was trapped. For seven weeks, little did we know, I was walking around with a collapsed lung!

The surgeon ordered a chest tube be put in and medication administered through the tube to break up the pockets. It was a grueling week, with return trips to the hospital every day to have the trapped fluid drained. At the end of the week, I underwent an outpatient procedure, a pleurodesis, to have my right lung coated with a solution to prevent future fluid buildup. During the procedure, I fell asleep, but I awoke with the most intense and excruciating pain I have ever felt in my life. I always believed I possessed a high tolerance for pain, but this time was significantly different. I began to hyperventilate, gasping for air, and couldn't stop shaking and crying. It took two rounds of strong painkillers to finally calm me down. Myron and I went home fatigued, praying this would be the end of fluid in my lungs and the answer to my condition.

God heard our prayers as I slowly began to heal over the course of the next several days, and I could breathe again. Feeling like I had new life, for the first time in weeks, I gulped in deep breaths! I felt my recovery was finally beginning. Myron and I gave thanks in humble and grateful praise to our God.

The journey to get where I am today was so hard and so difficult. While recuperating from my heart surgery, I slept in the living room on our sofa recliner. The fluid in my lung prevented me from reclining back or leaning forward. If I did, I would immediately begin to choke and feel like I was drowning. There were multiple sleepless nights as I sat straight up staring into the darkness. I listened to the tick-tock of the clock as the hours slowly crept by. Ten o'clock came and went, then 11 o'clock, midnight, 1 a.m., and 2 a.m. Sleep would not come. I felt alone and abandoned, and my mind was filled with questions of doubt. Sitting in the dark during those sleepless nights, the same conversation with God took place. It went something like this:

"Well, here I am again, Lord. Are You there? Will this ever be over? Will I ever sing again?" I asked.

Crickets.

Blackness.

Silence.

The silence was deafening, and the darkness was so black. I couldn't feel His presence. I was at the bottom of the pit. I didn't want to praise Him because God was too distant. Or was He? In the stillness of the night, I couldn't ignore God's still small voice.

"Judy, can you praise Me now?" I heard Him ask.

"No. I don't feel like it," I argued back.

And yet, God was there, extending His hand, reaching out to pull me from that black hole. Instead of feeling sorry for myself and for wallowing in self-pity, there was a clear choice to be made. I had to look up and take His hand. I had to seek the God I knew from the other hard times in my life. I continually had to choose to believe what I knew to be true, that God is good even when my circumstances aren't good. It was not without effort, but I decided to choose joy and began to praise Jesus every day. In reading God's Word, I looked for His Promises. In the Psalms, a precious verse spoke to me: "My flesh and my heart may fail, but God is the strength of my heart and my portion forever" (Psalm 73:26). Every day God gave me exactly what I needed. My heart was failing, and my lung was failing, but my God never failed me. He was always there.

Today, when I sit in the same spot on our sofa recliner, the memories of that dark time and place come flooding back. At first, it was difficult to sit there, but I am finding that to remember is a good thing. When I remember where God has brought me from, I can thank Him for it.

Should I live long enough, I'll face a second heart surgery. The cow valve that was used to replace my aortic valve will eventually wear out. I could choose to fret and worry about this future surgery, but why should I be afraid? God proved Himself so faithful during my first heart surgery that He won't fail me now! I proudly wear the jagged scar that runs down the center of my chest because it is a constant reminder of His faithfulness and His goodness to me!

When life is good and I bask in the goodness and sunshine of God's creation and sheer beauty of the earth, it's so easy to praise Him. But when the hard times hit, I struggled with praise. In the midst of my struggle, God changed me. There is something about being given two years to live that changes you. I'm not who I was. It's only by God's grace that I am still alive. I have seen God's unmerited favor, and every breath I take is a gift and spells purpose, which is to glorify Him. I'm blessed beyond what I ever deserve, and I am singing His praises once again. Even with all the heartache, my story is still being written.

It's pretty incredible to me that the Hebrew meaning of my name, Judith, is "praise." From these difficult experiences, my love for Christ is overflowing. How can I not praise Him? My praise is expressed in the following song that I wrote.

Praise

I gaze upon Your mountains, with their beauty I'm amazed.
And the vastness of the ocean, takes my breath away!
The wonder of all nature reminds me of Your Ways,
It makes me praise You all my days!

I look upon creation, and see Your Presence everywhere,
I feel Your love surround me as I breathe in fresh, clean air!
The wonder of Your Glory reminds me of Your Ways,
It's so easy to praise You all my days!
Oh, I will praise You all my days!

Then I face the hard times, feeling all alone.
Filled with doubt and sorrow, is my God still on the throne?
I can't feel Your arms around me, and there's no strength to pray.
How can I praise You all my days?
I've lost my praise for You today.

Sitting in the darkness, and I wonder where You are,
I rest upon Your promises; I know You're never far!
You reassure me by Your Spirit, You'll give me strength to carry on,
If I'll just praise You all my days,
Yes, choose to praise You all my days!

Cause You are here, always been, never left my side!
So I will trust all Your Ways. In You I will abide!
Cause even in the hard times, I know my God's still good.
You were with me in the darkness when I never understood,

So, I will praise You all my days!
Yes, keep on praising all my days!
Oh, I will praise You all my days!
I'll choose to praise You all my days!

Copyright © 2018 Judy Borntrager

9
GOD'S FINAL PIECE:
THE FINISHED WORK OF THE CROSS

"But you are a chosen people, a royal priesthood, a holy nation, God's special possession, that you may declare the praises of him who called you out of darkness into his wonderful light." (1 Peter 2:9)

EACH OF US has a story. My story, like yours, isn't over. God continues to write each chapter. I don't know your story. I don't know the anguish of the hard pieces in your puzzle or the times you've wanted to give up. Maybe you're angry with God because He has allowed horrific events to happen in your life that have left you distraught and feeling hopeless. Nevertheless, God does not change. From the hard things I've experienced in my own life, I've learned that He is not the source of my pain or difficult circumstances. We all have choices in this life. I had to choose how I would respond when I faced the pain that resulted from someone else's choices. I had to do the same when faced with grief, broken dreams of motherhood, and near-death experiences.

When your story is not going the way you think it should, look to the Author, Jesus. Let go of the pen, and stop attempting to write your own destiny. Embrace your story. Run to your Creator who loves you with an everlasting love. I have a personal relationship with the Author of my story. He's also the Author of your story, and I can assure you, He will complete it. The Bible promises us in Philippians that "Being confident of this, that he who began a good work in you will carry it on to completion until the day of Christ Jesus" (Philippians 1:6).

This book wasn't written because I have it all together, know all the answers, and have life figured out. I'm far from perfect. I still struggle and have questions about things I don't understand. A few years ago, I felt the Lord prompting me to tell my story. I argued with Him, saying, "I'm not educated enough. I'm not qualified. Please pick someone else!" But in choosing to be obedient to His calling, God uses me even when I feel so unworthy. Whenever I doubted, God was faithful to His promises and true to His Word. I choose to believe in Jesus, who believes in me. I'm grateful that I don't need to rely on my own strength to get through this life. I know that apart from Christ I am nothing. In Him, I simply want to preach what Jesus can do and shine His light to a lost, dark world. It's not always easy, and trusting Christ is a daily choice, but as I seek to abide in Jesus, He will lead me. His power living in me makes me who I am.

When we think our story has ended, God sees the big picture. He sees the final chapter. He will never leave you, and He certainly won't give up on you.

The Heart Condition We All Have

I was born with a physical heart condition that needed to be fixed, or I was going to die. Similarly, we're all born with a spiritual heart condition called sin. If we don't choose Jesus's payment for our sin and His gift of eternal life, we will die and be forever separated from God. But our story can be complete because of what Jesus did on the cross for us. Because He died for us and took our place, we have forgiveness of our sins. The Bible says, "For God so loved the world, that he gave his one and only Son, that whoever believes in him shall not perish but have eternal life" (John 3:16). God's Word continues, "If we confess our sins, he is faithful and just and will forgive us our sins and purify us from all unrighteousness" (1 John 1:9). Jesus not only died for our sins, but He arose on the third day, victorious over the grave! Because He lives, He conquered death! When our hope and trust is in Him, we have the promise of eternal life in heaven. Scripture reminds us, "For in him we live and move and have our being" (Acts 17:18).

Years ago, I made a promise to my father. It was Father's Day, and I had been asked to share something about my dad at our church. Standing in front of the congregation, I shared a piece of my story. Then I glanced over at my father who was sitting in his pew a few rows back. Looking him in the eye with tears streaming down my face, I said, "I promise I will be there, in heaven when I die. I promise not to miss it." Walking back to my seat, I approached my daddy's pew, where he stood up in the aisle, engulfed me in a great, big bear hug, and held me close.

Friends, I intend to keep that promise! Seeing Jesus in heaven is my final destiny where I can finally thank Him for all that He's done for me! I'm going to sprint through those pearly gates of heaven, looking for my dad who will once again wrap me in his arms and welcome me home! I'm anxious to see Darcy, who is not only walking on streets of gold as the Bible describes, but her eyes have been made whole, and she *sees* those streets of gold!

A Perfect Fit is only a fraction of my life's story. But as long as God gives me breath, and I am physically walking this earth, I am meant to live for Christ and to leave a legacy that glorifies Him. I'm confident every piece of the puzzle will fit. He's never made a mistake. If you haven't accepted Him, won't you join me in having a personal relationship with Jesus Christ by confessing your sins and your need for Him as the Savior of your life? Then, together, we can say with confidence:

"The LORD has done great things for us, and we are filled with joy" (Psalm 126:3).

If you appreciated *A Perfect Fit:*
The Work of the Master's Plan for the Puzzle of My Life,
kindly consider leaving a review at *Amazon* or *Goodreads*.

To hear Judy Zehr Borntrager sing
some of the songs mentioned in this book,
you can order her newly released album,
Praise,
which includes hymns and her original songs.

You may purchase CDs or download songs from the album at:
https://store.cdbaby.com/cd/judyborntrager

Praise is also available to download at CDBaby.com and through
Amazon, Pandora, Apple iTunes, and Spotify.

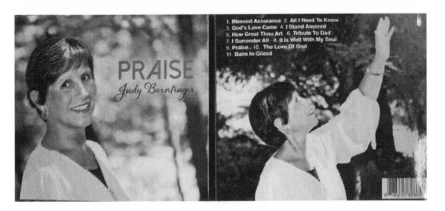

Judy-B-Praise

judyzehrborntrager.com

Updates on future publications can be found at:

GROUND TRUTH PRESS
P.O. Box 7313
Nashua, NH 03060-7313

www.groundtruthpress.com

Made in the USA
Monee, IL
28 February 2020